Inward Apocalypse

"*Inward Apocalypse* is a timely invitation to readers to develop their faith for the common good. The book's refreshing honesty—even about the growing pains of faith—allows readers to rest in the well-earned wisdom of a trusted guide and confidant. Howard writes with depth, insight, and authenticity, weaving together personal experiences, poetry, and compelling scholarship to reveal a theology that is actually good news for the entire community of creation."

—AMY KENNY
author of *My Body Is Not a Prayer Request*

"*Inward Apocalypse* is a gift to all who long for faith with power to ground us in these shifting times. With clarity, wit, and surprising insight, Howard drops gems as she leads readers through apocalypse to the common good."

—LISA SHARON HARPER
author of *Fortune: How Race Broke my Family and the World and How to Repair it All*

"*Inward Apocalypse* is smart, witty, and captivating. I could not put it down. Howard's thinking and writing are as solid as can be, compelling us to pilgrimage alongside her as she confronts the toxic Christian subculture and theology in which many are steeped. Howard raises thought-provoking questions and challenges American Christians who seek to follow the Jesus of the Gospels and not the Jesus of our national imagination."

—MARLENA GRAVES
author of *The Way Up Is Down: Becoming Yourself by Forgetting Yourself*

"Howard weaves together vivid personal experience and rich theological reflection. Her voice in *Inward Apocalypse* is a steady, faithful guide for any who have found themselves out of sorts or tightly bound by the story of God they were given. Through recounting her own moments of disruption, Howard invites readers to find their way through their own such moments and encounter a more expansive, beautiful, and transformative faith."

—MEGAN WESTRA
author of *Born Again and Again*

"*Inward Apocalypse* offers us hope and a roadmap so that we can restore the common good together. If you've ever found yourself disoriented or disturbed by the scandals or misuse of power by clergy leaders, this book is for you. You will feel seen, cared for, and loved— this book is a well of healing."

—ASHLEY ABERCROMBIE
author of *Love Is the Resistance*

"In this meditation and memoir, Anna Howard shares the complex reality of journeying from her childhood faith towards an ever-deepening understanding of Christ, justice, challenge, and hope. This brilliant book is a must-read for anyone asking the hard questions about rediscovering faith when one realizes that the suppositions, hierarchies, and -isms built into one's story of faith cannot stand."

—YEJIDE PETERS
Berkeley Divinity School

INWARD APOCALYPSE

Uncovering a faith for the common good

ANNA ELISABETH HOWARD

RESOURCE *Publications* • Eugene, Oregon

INWARD APOCALYPSE
Uncovering a Faith for the Common Good

Copyright © 2022 Anna Elisabeth Howard. All rights reserved. Except for brief quotations in critical publications or reviews, no part of this book may be reproduced in any manner without prior written permission from the publisher. Write: Permissions, Wipf and Stock Publishers, 199 W. 8th Ave., Suite 3, Eugene, OR 97401.

Wipf & Stock
An Imprint of Wipf and Stock Publishers
199 W. 8th Ave., Suite 3
Eugene, OR 97401

www.wipfandstock.com

PAPERBACK ISBN: 978-1-6667-3581-9
HARDCOVER ISBN: 978-1-6667-9328-4
EBOOK ISBN: 978-1-6667-9329-1

Scripture quotations are from New Revised Standard Version Bible, copyright © 1989 National Council of the Churches of Christ in the United States of America. Used by permission. All rights reserved worldwide.

Book Design by Anna Elisabeth Howard
Cover tree illustration by Pavel Konovalov

To my readers:
May you begin.

Contents

Introduction ix

Section One: Beginnings 1

1: Fire 3

2: Chrysalis 15

3: Judas 29

4: Creation 41

5: Mother 55

Section Two: Embodiment 67

6: Emmaus 69

7: Pilgrim 79

8: Numbers 91

9: Broken 101

10: Hurt 115

Section Three: Fulfillment 125

11: Sick 127

12: Other	143
13: Extraction	153
14: Story	167
15: Renewed	179
Acknowledgements	189
Bibliography	191
About the Author	197

Introduction

When I was a little girl and was afraid of the dark, I would ask Jesus to come sit on my bed and hold my hand while I fell asleep. I'd lay there with my hand outstretched firmly believing that he was right there in the dark with me. Even as I grew older, I used to believe that God spoke to me directly and not only cared about all the little details of my life, but intervened in them. I would pray for answers to all kinds of things from parking places for class to major life decisions. Somewhere around my first crisis of faith, I stopped doing this. By the time I reached what I could define as a dark night of the soul, I'd stopped praying all together as there didn't seem to be a point. My prayers felt like they stopped at the ceiling and I no longer had a sense that Jesus was sitting with me in the dark.

And yet God didn't stop finding ways to get my attention. At least, it seems that way, but I prefer to stay somewhat agnostic about it all. That being said, after having the same conversation with multiple people within a year's time, I thought maybe something was trying to get my attention.

The conversation goes something like this: "I used to be a Christian. I was raised _____ [fill in the blank with some evangelical to fundamentalist church or tradition]. But I don't believe any of that anymore."

Then there's usually a pause. Sometimes I would murmur something about understanding feeling that way because I've been there too. And then the person would turn to me and say something along the lines of "but I wish I could still believe in God, I just don't know how to do that any more."

I had a conversation with my friend Alexandra as the first draft of this book was being birthed and she told me that she too was writing a book. And she'd prayed about it, but instead of asking for permission, she'd just said, "Okay God, I'm doing this and I need your help." She'd listened to a video from Glennon Doyle about how to know when you're a writer and something clicked. Glennon I'm pretty sure would say that Alexandra had found her knowing[1]. And see, I think that the knowing is God.

If we are created in God's image, then learning to listen to our knowing is learning to listen to God and we can trust that. This will probably set off some inner speech for folks because it's directly opposite to what we--especially women--have been taught for most of our lives by the church and by society, but it's the wounds of the church in this regard that often hurt the most.

But if you're up for the task of learning to question everything and then probably question it all again, I'll tell you the tale of my two crises of faith, three dark nights of the soul, and finding a faith I could still believe in on the other side. And more than a faith that I could believe for myself, the faith I came back to is a faith for the common good: a faith that points to total thriving and well-being for everyone and how we can build that world together, a concept Lisa Sharon Harper calls the very good gospel.

My hope is along the way you'll start to tell your own story as well because our stories have so much power in them. Perhaps you're already there and that's why you picked up this book: your questions and doubts have built to a crescendo and refuse to be ignored. It's dark; it's scary; and it seems endless right now. However, I am firmly convinced the way to freedom lies in peeling back all the layers of bad theology and finding what it means to pursue God's shalom.

Ready? Here we go.

---

[1] See Glennon Doyle, *Untamed*, for Glennon's discussion of finding and learning to trust your "knowing."

Section One: Beginnings

approach my trauma
carefully
declare it holy ground
take off your sandals
and sit before it
in silent contemplation
the time will come
when god-fire
rushes down
watch it burn
but not consume
me
now watch god
perform
a miracle
turning trauma
to truth
which i will then use
to part the beliefs
that once held me
captive
so let me go
preacher and
pharaoh
i am not
a plague
sent to annoy
your faith
or an exodus
sent to trouble
your church
but a woman with a song
and a long walk
to a promised land
flowing with
respect
and equality

—Kaitlin Shetler

1

Fire

I pour the beans into the grinder and the sharp, rich smell of coffee fills my nostrils as I replace the lid and grind the beans into small, usable grounds to be immolated in boiling water and transformed into something usable for me to drink. And then it hits me. I used to have a faith where God was the coffee grinder and the boiling water and I was supposed to be grateful for the grinding and the burning and the transformation because God was God and God's ways were higher than mine so who was I to question?

I was eight or nine years old and my parents had led me up to an "altar call" of some sort at a "camp meeting" in Louisiana. This was an indoor camp-meeting, the air-conditioning protecting us from both the floral-scented, sticky summer air of Baton Rouge and outsiders. The way I understood it, camp-meeting was supposed to be about the gospel, but this one seemed to just attract followers of the preacher who held these. Instead of a general call to a community, this was a pilgrimage for the extra-holy, charismatic-type, loosely or not so loosely associated with the Assemblies of God denomination.

I wasn't in need of "getting saved," and I don't think that's even what this altar call was about. If you hear my parents tell it, I had taken care of the salvation thing by making an individual choice to pray the sinner's prayer at the age of three. Though how in the name of all of child psychology a three-year-old is making any kind of independent decision of that magnitude, I'll never know. This time it was to get prayed over for something. All I remember is staring at the wide midsection of the pastor in front of me as he laid his hands on my head and prayed: "give her a call to Africa, God, give her a call to Africa."

I went back to my seat perturbed. I didn't want to go to Africa, but even at that tender age, I'd gotten the message loud and clear that God would just do with my life what God wanted: not what I wanted. And even though my parents had the sense to tell me that just because he prayed that didn't mean God was calling me to be a missionary, this stayed with me for years. I was going to go to Africa: specifically what was still called Zaire, now the DRC, right in the heart of the continent. I had decided on that country after praying over a map, and then I spent much time researching it until I was thirteen or so.

You see, this faith I was being raised in required us to be molded by God in uncomfortable and often painful ways. No mention of life doing this just fine all by itself, and then maybe our faith as a tool to get us through that. No. It was all God. God was all-powerful and worked all things together for our good, but the main message was God was doing the working; God was doing the initiating.

This faith was also laden with subtext. Here we were a bunch of mostly white people gathered together, and the white man praying over me speaks of Africa as this monolithic place that I'm supposed to go to. Because that's what women with calls to ministry did: they became overseas missionaries. We weren't fit to preach the gospel to white men, but to those "other people," you know, the Black and brown ones, those we could preach to.

And thus the gospel given to me at that tender age was presented in the putrid wrappings of misogyny, racism, and an inherently colonialistic mindset that was for some unexamined and for some intentional. I would carry these weights for a long time before I had the tools to examine what I'd been given and then ask myself: "What if I stopped believing all of this? What would it look like to take these wrappings off the gospel? What would be left, and can I still believe it?"

Of course, these questions didn't present themselves in tidy packages to be answered. It would take the better part of the second twenty years of my life to answer them. I would walk away and walk back more than once before finding a place where my faith helped me make sense of the world and was nourishing to me instead of harmful.

FIRE

***

I was sixteen years old and attending yet another large mega church, this one in Colorado Springs. The youth group got together every Wednesday night, and I remember being on my knees during worship, hands in the air, singing out "refiner's fire, my heart's one desire, is to be holy, set apart for you my master, ready to do your will." The youth group at this point was one of my few escapes from a toxic family life, but surely that was all God's doing right? God's refining fire?

The really god-hungry among us teenagers also attended the Sunday night services together, sitting in a section of the church where we were somehow away from all the adults for the most part, as if our habit of sitting there had caused that section to be reserved; or, maybe it was just because it was in the front, I don't know. Here we listened to sermons from the pastor and associate pastor, both white men again, surrounded by pretty much all white folks again, sitting in a warehouse-style building where the flags of the world hung from the exposed metal rafters thirty feet above our heads. The sermons revolved around missions, prayer, spiritual mapping, and the 10-40 window: this area of the world between 10 degrees and 40 degrees latitude where supposedly resided the most people who had never heard the gospel. Oh, and a bunch about the sin of homosexuality as this was the late 1990's and that was a really big thing to preach about in these white evangelical circles.

This white, male, straight, able-bodied gospel was the default. The rest of us that didn't literally fit that definition had to find a way to mold ourselves around it, no matter how much it hurt. Evidently, when you're white, straight, able-bodied, and male you get to be part of doing the molding instead of always on the receiving end and no one bats an eye.

***

Later in seminary, I took a theology and film class and one of the assigned movies was *Saved*. My father was working from home at the time, and often watched the movies with me as I completed my homework. I remember his incredulity at the ending.

"So it's the adulterous pastor, the unwed mother, the Jewish atheist, and gay boyfriend?" He scoffed as the characters gathered around the hospital bed to admire the new baby.

I looked at him out of the corner of my eye and said, "Yeah, I think that's what the kingdom of God looks like."

And he was so astounded, he didn't have an answer for me.

I went on for a while after that still thinking I had to believe that marriage equality was somehow not biblical until one day I realized I didn't want to believe that any more. And I thought, what if I just stopped? I put down that heavy weight of a belief that I thought I had to keep defending and realized not only was it the loving thing to do, but it freed me up in the process.

Ultimately, I ended up in a process of deconstruction where I pulled apart each tiny bit of faith and set it aside to be examined. Most of it got discarded. What I ended up with was far lighter and infinitely richer than what I'd started with. I thought the fire was supposed to burn me; but, it turns out it burned away everything I didn't need. I was left with all that I couldn't leave behind, as U2 sings in "Walk On," a song and an album that was released right before I started at Fuller Theological Seminary in Pasadena, CA in the winter of 2001, and subsequently became a soundtrack for that section of my life in more ways than one. It didn't hurt that one of my Old Testament professors was a huge U2 fan, even titling one of his books after that song.

"And love is not the easy thing / The only baggage you can bring / Is all that you can't leave behind."

Most of what I was taught before the age of twenty turned out to be baggage of the most damaging kind. It was not only unnecessary weight, it obscured the gospel and the image of God both in others and in me. I didn't feel worthy when I looked in the mirror. I didn't see myself as beloved because of intrinsic worth, created in the image of God. I had imbibed the message that God loves me because of God's qualities, not because of mine.

Matt Nightingale wrote a twitter thread on the evangelical prooftext Jeremiah 17:9: "The heart is deceitful above all things and beyond cure. Who can understand it?" He pointed out how evangelical and fundamentalist Christianity teaches that we have to minimize our feelings. And not just our feelings, our questions. We are supposed to blindly accept the faith as handed down to us by these white, male pastors. If we have questions, we're supposed to discard them and trust. After all, we can't trust our hearts, so we have to trust the bible and the pastor. Only the bible was written by people with these same supposedly deceitful hearts, and the pastor, well, isn't he (because in these contexts, it's pretty much always "he") in possession of one of these fickle organs as well? But the possession of white maleness seemed to be an edge over the fickleness.

***

One Sunday after church, I was standing in the courtyard, and I overheard two middle-aged women talking to each other about male leadership. One of them said she was convinced that women weren't supposed to be pastors because she was just "all over the place" and it took her husband's beliefs to bring her in line. Something inside my twenty-year-old self cringed. But I'd been taught not to trust that internal cringing. I had a conversation later that year with another twenty-something woman where we confessed that we ourselves were uncomfortable with female senior pastors. We both had clear inclinations toward ministry. I was staying over with her at her apartment because we were running the vacation bible school that year. She was employed by the church in the children's ministry department. I was about to start seminary.

The image of God in us had been so eroded in our own minds that we had bought into the lie that we were less-than. That refiner's fire was supposed to burn away everything "not-god" within us but it had turned into something that had stolen the essential truth of the gospel away from us. We could no longer see ourselves as the image of God, not fully, not equally. That had been burned away, and we thought it was good.

In one of her first works on understanding shame, Brené Brown writes, "Power-over is a dangerous form of power. Dr. Robin Smith, a psychologist and contributor to *The Oprah Winfrey Show*, described one of the most insidious forms of power-over as working like this:

'I will define who you are, and then I'll make you believe that's your own definition.' This chilling explanation of power-over captures what shame does to us. It forces us into gender straitjackets; then convinces us we put them on ourselves, and that we enjoy wearing them."[1] These "gender straitjackets" are exactly what my friend and I were wearing, and we felt daring because we were insistent on keeping them on ourselves.

***

Several years after I got married, in the midst of wanting a baby, experiencing a miscarriage, and subsequent trouble conceiving, I had a dream I had a baby. In this dream, I went to the church with the baby, and I thought, "now I'll finally fit in." As a woman and the female spouse of a male clergy person, there were still all these unwritten expectations that seemed a heavy subtext in many conversations I had with parishioners. Would I join the choir? Help with Sunday School? And when was I going to have a baby? It wasn't enough that I had achieved marriage and eliminated that question. I would not be "complete" until I had children too. And yes, children because it only took until my first child was six months old for me to be asked if I was thinking of having another one.

I'm sure if I had directly challenged any of these with the question, "Am I not enough on my own?" the church ladies and others would have either not known how to answer or would have affirmed that of course I was enough on my own. I didn't "have" to be married or have children to be a complete woman, and yet these questions wore on me even as I tried to remind myself that they came from a place of image-erosion that had occurred in these women as well.

Generations of women are convinced that we put the straitjacket on ourselves, and in turn we help convince other women to wear it too. Unless. Unless we accept our belovedness on our own accounts. Unless we dare to believe that God made us equally in her image. Only then can we throw off the straitjackets. As we get free and tell our stories, we help others walk into freedom alongside us.

---
[1] Brené Brown, *I Thought It Was Just Me (but it isn't)*, 24.

FIRE

There are precious few women with names and whole stories in the Bible. One of the most prominent ones is one that in my upbringing was also the most controversial, which makes perfect sense if you think about it. All powerful women in the Bible had to be subverted so that we modern women wouldn't get any ideas that powerful women were "biblical." This particular woman is Mary, the mother of Jesus. Nadia Bolz-Weber talks about how "Mary got precious little mention in my religious upbringing apart from our sneering at people (like Roman Catholics) who 'worshiped' her. To us, Mary was little more than a minor character in the Christmas story and to pay any more attention to her than that was to inch dangerously toward Catholic idolatry. Sure, Mary could be admired for her obedience, but we knew better than to turn Mary into some kind of golden calf—that which the mistaken, the lost, and the ignorant worship instead of God."[2]

Like Nadia, I was raised in a tradition that looked askance at Roman Catholics and declared that, because of "Mary-worship" among other things, they weren't even "real Christians." Mary's story was told quickly in the context of Jesus' birth. She was held up as an example for obedience and motherhood and left at that. It was a long time before I could consider that there was more to the story. You see Nadia and I and thousands upon thousands of other girls had been taught that we were not worthy. That we were not to trust ourselves. And while some would argue that this was the general teaching to everyone in these evangelical or fundamentalist church groups, there was a special level of unworthiness ascribed to women in both spoken and unspoken ways. After all, it was Eve who ate the apple. We were "less" and the only way to atone for this was to accept our "biblical" roles and train other women to do the same thing. Eventually, by the time of our deaths, we might have done enough to appease God the father and thereby worked out our salvation.

"Being a woman in a great many versions of religious traditions can be varying shades of a negative personal trait," writes Teresa Mateus. "It can limit what you can do in a religious community and culture, if you are allowed to talk and what you are allowed to say or are considered capable of saying... This again is seen as a theme in issues of historic abuse and colonization, sexual identity negation,

---
2 Nadia Bolz Weber, *Accidental Saints*, 66.

and more."³ And if simply being born female needs to be rendered in a negative light, then the few stories of women in the Bible have to have their legs cut out from under them.

But what if we looked at Mary's story another way? What if it's not her obedience and submissiveness and motherhood that make her special? What if it's because she dared to trust that she was really highly favored by God. As Nadia put it, "Maybe the really outrageous act of faith on Mary's part was trusting that she had found favor with God. I may feel used to the idea that if I live a certain kind of life, I can make myself worthy of God. But what if God's Word is so much more powerful than our ability to become worthy of God? I mean, not for nothing, but if God can create the universe by speaking it into existence, then I think God can make us into God's beloved by simply saying it is so."⁴

If we are created in God's image—all of us of all genders, ethnicities, and cultures—then I don't think it's a big stretch to say that we are intrinsically worthy because of that. A Facebook friend posted one of those Christian-y memes that said something like, "God loves us because of who God is, not because of who we are." And of course, that is true because God's nature is Love. However that is not the whole story. We are intrinsically worthy of love as well and believing this doesn't negate the truth about the nature of God.

God's love isn't an aspect of God: God is love--wholly, completely, unselfishly. And God's love in perfection unlike our broken understandings of it isn't predicated or dependent or conditional upon the actions or response of anyone. This Love is the actual divine fire that we encounter in Scripture, an all encompassing love that defies the boundaries even of the words we use to try to come to some understanding of it. To know God is to know Love, and yet we cannot comprehend it fully and so we try to remake God's love into an image that we can understand.

We stand our view of our own unworthiness up against God's perfection and make statements about the love of God while self-flagellating in what we think is a necessary recognition of our sinfulness. "God loves us despite our unworthiness," we think is a

---

3 Teresa B. Pasquale, *Healing Spiritual Wounds*, 108.
4 Nadia Bolz Weber, *Accidental Saints*, 69.

statement extolling God and yet this devaluing of God's creation is not a compliment to the Creator. God loves because God is, this is one reality not two. And being created in God's image imparts worthiness to the creation, this is one reality not two.

To know God is to know Love. To say we follow this Love is to commit to embody love ourselves. And this is not an unnatural state for humans, or trying to force our "sinful flesh" to behave contrary to our nature: rather this is a return to our true nature as created by Love. All of our understanding of God and ourselves comes back to and is encompassed by this reality. For as Katherine Sonderegger puts it, "Divine Attributes that cannot be recognized as restatements, better, as harmonics, of Love can never lead to true and full and healing knowledge of God."[5] And she goes on to say that "A doctrine of God that does not call a reader to love, does not remind one of the tang and taste of love, does not draw one back in to the saltiness of love, human and divine, cannot serve the Lord well, but is a servant without profit."[6]

To say we know God and follow God is to make a bold statement about living encompassed by and out of Love. We cannot say that we know God if we deny the full and complete humanity of any human. To do so is to deny the image of God and the very nature of God. We cannot love while creating a hierarchy among humans. To do so attempts to place conditions upon God's love and attempts to break apart the very nature of God into something that not only can be fully grasped within our minds, but also controlled and used for control of others. Creating a hierarchy makes God's love conditional and sets ministers and others in "special" roles as potential mediators of that love. In this view, God's fire becomes a refining fire that burns away our unworthiness, and who needs more refining is defined and dictated by the very ones that should be serving the least of these.

This is a perverted view of God for God's love has no conditions: it simply is. Going back to Sonderegger, "Should we imagine that we could live as those unscathed and uncharred by Divine Love—loveless citizens of an icy and indifferent world—and yet know God, we are deceived."[7] This is God's fire. And rather than a refining fire to burn

---
5 Katherine Sonderegger, *Systematic Theology, Volume 1*, 471.
6 *Ibid*, 471.
7 *Ibid*, 471.

away our unworthiness, it calls us to abide in God's very self—Love—and to live out of that Love towards our fellow humans. This fire does not subtract; rather, it heals our brokenness and completes our understanding and ability to live in Love.

***

It's been about twenty-five years since I sat down at the piano and learned the basics of music theory, seemingly the most boring part of learning music, and yet it is the foundation for every musical expression. The rigors of the theory give freedom to the creativity because it allows one to understand the pieces that make music work. The very idea of harmonics is tied to a mathematical ratio, without which, the music would be off and not be pleasing to our ears or resonate with our souls. The combination of certain harmonics within a musical instrument is what gives a particular instrument its timbre or its voice.

Harmonics are essential to producing music. They are definable and predictable from the standpoint that only certain physical attributes of musical instruments cause them to be properly produced. Trying to make a musical instrument without understanding the math and physics around the production of harmonics results in flat, off tones that sound bad and produce a chaotic listening experience, if such a thing can still be called music and if we can stand to listen to it.

In the same way, failure to understand that all divine attributes can be recognized as harmonics of love, produces doctrinal points that sound chaotic and flat because they are inconsistent and out of harmony with God and with the well-being of the humans they claim to benefit. All of the ways we live out faith should also be recognizable as harmonics of love. And this love cannot elevate one category of people above the others as worthy recipients of love by comparison to another category. Doctrine that only elevates a single category of people and turns them into a wedge to be used against other people, or say a single issue at the ballot box, isn't true doctrine because it is not in harmony with love.

God's relentless, unconditional delight in and love for human beings must be our standard by which we measure all doctrine and belief. This delight and love leads to seeking the best interest of all people, so that all people can mutually thrive and no one is left out. This goes beyond any bare legal definitions of equality and seeks to truly love our neighbors as ourselves.

I am from Sitka spruces and glacier melt streams
    toes wriggling on the beach rocks
    that split my lip as I learned to walk
I am from baked chicken and rice and
    candied carrots
swimming in brown sugar juices
I am from loneliness and isolation
    and from all the lives I've lived
    in books I've read
I am from Nancy and Amy
    from Rachel and Sarah
    and Madeleine and Sue
I am from pine groves and long grass
    secret dens next to the vast webs
    field spiders wove
I am from a branch of rotten wood
    toxic gospel and white supremacy
    from dogma that mattered more
    than people
I am from paint palettes and watercolors
    and colorful brushstrokes
    that belied a "color-blind" existence
I am from sushi and thai food
    and a graft made to save my life
and my faith
I am from dark nights and slow walks
    from u-turns and grace
    and from the family I found and made
        –Anna Elisabeth Howard

2

Chrysalis

I was twenty-one and sitting in an Old Testament class at Fuller Theological Seminary, staring at Genesis like I'd never read it before. There are two different creation narratives and this is the truth that starts to set me free. If there could be multiple writers of Genesis, then what else had I grown up believing that I didn't need to hold onto any longer? And then I moved on to the well-worn fall narrative, you know the one where Eve eats the apple and damns all of humanity? Well, much to my surprise, Adam was right there too. She didn't run off and trick him as I'd been taught whether explicitly or implicitly; rather, he was standing there listening to the whole conversation.

Seminary was the first chrysalis. I wasn't aware of it being so at the time, but is the caterpillar really sure of what it's doing when it enters the chrysalis? Or is it just drawn by some instinct? I can't speak for the caterpillar; but for me, it was definitely the latter.

I was just out of college and had been volunteering for two years with a fifth and sixth grade ministry at yet another mega church, this one in the San Fernando Valley in Los Angeles. We ran this ministry like a miniature youth group, and it formed the bridge between what I'd perceived as a call to children's ministry, and the decision to enter a youth ministry program at Fuller. It was also my first experience of being the only woman on an all-male team and having my ideas dismissed only to later be slightly edited and stolen by one of the men on the team. When I brought it up with the staff member, he laughed at me and dismissed that it was happening even though I had clear examples.

The divide between what I was trying to do with my contributions to this ministry and what I was learning in seminary only grew, leading me to accept a friend's invitation to help chaperon the junior high retreat with an eye towards coming on staff at the church she was working at. It was an immersion experience in more ways than one as she worked at an immigrant Taiwanese congregation with the English congregation who at that time were the junior high to college age kids, mostly 1.5 to 2nd generation Chinese immigrants. That retreat was my first experience of being the only white person in the room and at first I was aware of it. The staff at the retreat center who were all white as I recall seemed to stare at me, but I'm not sure whether they actually did or if I was hyper aware of myself in that moment.

The feeling of awkwardness didn't last for me anyway, I felt very accepted very quickly, and I don't remember ever feeling again like people were looking at me on outings where I was the only white person in the group.

Deciding to accept the job at my friend's church was one of the ways I became aware of the casual racism I'd been raised with. In many ways, it wasn't overt. But, when I said I wanted to go work at this church, I got push back from some family members. They were afraid in that context I either wouldn't get married, or I'd marry a Chinese guy. It was a repeated theme in my early twenties. After all, that was my job as a woman: get married and have kids. And while there's nothing wrong with that, I had never seen myself as on a track to do "only" that. I'd been raised in a culture where "what do you want to do when you grow up?" when asked of girls, no one batted an eye if we answered "just want to be a mommy." And yet, I never heard little boys say they "just" wanted to be daddies. In fact, it was assumed little boys hadn't thought about it, and it was weird even if boys talked about their future families. Girls were supposed to be obsessed with it; boys were supposed to grow into it as men. Now, raising two little boys of my own, both of them have talked about having kids when they grow up amidst other things they want to do, and it seems perfectly natural. But I digress.

Putting myself in a situation where I was the only white person gave me a lens to examine our culture: both the whiteness I was raised with and that surrounds all of us, and what it looks like to live life as a non-white person within the United States. It also gave me a first-hand introduction to immigrants. These questions of immigration weren't abstract for me: they literally affected people I knew. Immigrants weren't a class of people to be dealt with en masse; they were individuals with hopes and dreams and stories just as real as mine.

It would be another ten years or so before I started unpacking the realities of anti-Black and anti-indigenous racism in this country and the different tone and tenor those take. My experience as the only white person in the room gave me a handhold to look at race that helped me continue parsing all of it.

***

The carpet in the family room where the toys were was orange. It may have been the late nineteen-eighties at this point, but the seventies still reigned in this room. Our legos covered a large folding table set up by the window and opposite that stood a bookshelf with some books and a basket of matchbox cars. I don't know for sure what else was on the bookshelf, but one prized possession was a much-read copy of The Picture Bible held together by duct tape. My formative years were defined by this particular book so much that it took me a long time to question the pictures from it. These pictures formed my mental images of the people in the Bible well into young adulthood. One look at the table of contents reveals the stories deemed important by the author are about Abraham, Moses, David, Jesus, and Paul. Ruth and Esther are the only women who get their own sections. Of course, this isn't exactly the fault of the author, the weight of the stories in scripture lend to this skewed percentage as well. One has to look at the overall trajectory of the Bible to see equality and liberation as a theme.

During the writing of this, I listened in on a webinar which was a conversation about decolonizing the gospel between Lisa Sharon Harper and René August.[1] Lisa spoke of a time when she felt repulsed by the Bible even while believing the truth of it because of the layers of whiteness in which the Bible had been presented to her. And I resonated with that, mentally adding, "and maleness!" While it might

---
1 Lisa Sharon Harper and René August, "How to Decolonize the Bible."

seem more obvious that I want to unpack the maleness of the text, it also matters that I unpack the way in which the Bible has been presented as white.

I purchased a used copy of the Picture Bible off eBay to get a new look at what was so formative in my childhood. Most of the characters are presented with very European features. David is blonde. Jesus has wavy medium brown hair and pale skin. There's little in these cartoons that would have told my early self literally none of these people were of European descent. The exception being the people who were the "bad guys" in the story: the ones who didn't believe Noah, the people of Sodom and Gomorrah. These people are almost unfailingly depicted with dark curly hair, dark eyes, and often with darker skin tones. The gospel available to me as a child had been appropriated by European colonists as surely as the land itself in what would be called the United States. Mixed in with the "good news" of Jesus was the implicit teaching that white was good and brown and Black were not.

The biggest catalyst that pushed my anti-racism journey to another level where I ended up actively working on myself to peel back the layers of systemic racism in my heart was when Trayvon Martin was murdered in 2012, and his killer was allowed to go free. It shook me to my core. Here was this beautiful kid, just like so many I had taught in various youth ministries at various churches, and his life had been stolen. And then our "justice" system said it wasn't a crime.

Around that time a couple of friends of mine became very vocal on Facebook about race, and their lived experiences as Black persons in the United States. I sat at their feet virtually and listened. For a long time, they had no idea, which is one of the beauties of social media. It gave me space to process all my feelings about whiteness without ever saying anything to them.

I began to realize that whiteness is an assumed identity. Most of us of European descent are baptized into it by our parents. Ironic really, coming from traditions that looked disdainfully on the practice of baptizing infants into the Christian faith, so many white fundamentalists baptize their children into whiteness without batting an eye. Whiteness as an identity was chosen long before the identity even of "American." When the European colonists found themselves outnumbered by both indigenous people and stolen African people, they abandoned their identities as English, Dutch, German, French, and so on, and instead created the idea of whiteness.[2] With this action they both created supremacy on the basis of skin tone and removed all people of European descent from their individual traditions and heritage too. Maintaining power was to be the sole unifier, and the colonists sold their identities to do it.

In *I'm Still Here: Black Dignity in a World Made for Whiteness*, Austin Channing Brown talks about her experience meeting Black Jesus and how that was transformative for her as a black woman.[3] But this white woman also needed to meet Jesus as he really was: a brown, indigenous person, colonized by an empire, lynched by the state for his justice work, betrayed by religious leaders for his perceived blasphemy. The gospel I'd been introduced to where a savior with flowing brown hair and pale skin was crucified for my individual sins was not only a tiny gospel, but a perverse one.

Raised in this white, American Christianity that proclaimed that Jesus died to give the American definition of liberty and justice to all, I was insulated for a long time from the reality that it failed miserably to do any of that for "all." Liberty was only guaranteed to a select few that were almost uniformly white, male, and rich. Probably most of them were also straight and able-bodied as well. And American justice propped up by this theology became about imprisoning people who society rejects: people who are poor or addicted or people of color or mentally ill. Almost no one who our American "justice" system has labeled as criminals is dangerous to anyone.

I grew up in mostly white churches who sent missionaries to the benighted heathens of South America and Africa (and yes, those were monolithic continents all too often), being taught affirmative action was "reverse racism," and the expectations that nice white girls grew up to marry nice white boys and raise another generation of babies to baptize into this worldview.

***

---

2 See Lisa Sharon Harper, *Fortune*, 37-53.
3 Austin Channing Brown, *I'm Still Here*, 37-39.

I frame seminary as the first chrysalis because I feel like I've done this cycle multiple times: the enclosing and emerging happening over and over because there is just so much to unpack. Anti-indigenous racism was a more recent layer for me to examine and as I look at that I can see the roots reaching back into what I was raised with both with the inherent white supremacy and the idea that environmentalists made the planet an idol, and thus the idea we needed to conserve it was inherently wrong. The idea of Mother Earth was wrapped up and discarded as idolatrous in the same breath Mary was thrown out as suspect and Roman Catholics dismissed as "not really Christian" because of her.

Baptism represents the waters of creation, the waters of the womb, but I was baptized into a culture of white, male supremacy. And what does that mean? If femaleness is removed from the gospel and the Godhead, the baptismal font is rendered little more than an artificial womb: cold, metallic, and lacking connection to the living source.

All mother connections were discarded, and I was left with a Father God who knew better than I did what to do with my life. I was supposed to shut up and not ask questions. After all, questions are doubt, and people of faith don't do that. This faith as it was handed to me was small and self-contained, lacking all the connections to faith of people in the era between the early church and the Reformation and was presented in a barely veiled self-congratulatory light for being the faith that "got it right" whether looking at how the Jewish people "missed it"—antisemitism anyone?—to the Roman church "perverting it," and thus being "not Christian."

It may seem as though I've already circled some of the same topics, but what I'm hoping to show you is how I had to circle around multiple times, peeling back layers, unraveling threads, and then putting new threads on the loom to reweave a faith I could believe in. One of the threads that felt real was this reconnection to various kinds of mother and intrinsically female imagery. This imagery is actually represented in the text of Scripture, but is skimmed over and has its power snatched away every time it occurs. Reclaiming these texts reclaims multiple threads, and begins to weave a new and much more robust tapestry.

I love the phrase "divine feminine." It feels like coming home. Or I should say, it feels like that now. Years ago it would have conjured something different, something pagan and forbidden and wholly divorced from things "good Christians" should believe in. The divine feminine, Mother Earth, mother Mary, and other images of femaleness associated with God, creation, and our faith had been violently excised from the faith I was raised with. Bringing forward arguments in history over whether women had souls, or if they could be fully saved, the idea we couldn't be pastors was just the latest iteration of a deeply misogynistic gospel that has done violence to countless women.

The pandemic showed me that one can get used to all sorts of things. The first month or so I had a lot of anxiety about it all, but as we rounded the corner on the third month of basically staying quarantined, I had sort of come to terms with it. Did I want it to be over? Of course. But the level of anxiety had reduced as I became accustomed to living with this new reality.

In the case of a pandemic, this is a useful survival tool. In the case of the injustices in our society, it is the opposite. Well, the opposite in terms of shalom for everyone anyway. Sure, it shields white people and male people and straight people and abled people, etc. And it is not a safe thing to question any of these permutations of the status quo because the people they benefit the most—the people who hold more than their share of power—will fight against that questioning.

***

My oldest child was about three years old at most, and I was standing in the doorway of the tiny nursery at the church where my husband was the rector (Episcopal-speak for the pastor). One of the older men had tried to get him to do something he didn't want to do, I don't even remember what—a high five or a hug or something perhaps—and instead of making my son ignore his own boundaries and do something conciliatory towards the adult, I emphasized that he didn't have to do whatever it was. I was physically blocking the door at this point, not because this person was some kind of predator; but because they were operating out of the assumption that kids were supposed to do what adults wanted, and it was okay to make them. The man was irritated at that point and made a comment about "getting those apron strings cut." I seethed. There was much loaded into this comment, implying my preschooler needed to be set free from his mother in order to grow into a real man or something along those lines.

That's not the first time I've seen it implied that "mother" is something you outgrow. Mother Earth isn't something we discuss because that's an idol. People are more important than plants and animals after all. As though we aren't all interconnected, and at the very least, we need the survival of the earth in order to support our own life on this planet. But even such self-centered logic is lost on many who grew up reciting a pledge of allegiance to a floppy bit of fabric, a lifeless and manufactured symbol we were trained to revere, while allegiance to the planet that helped birth us was wrong. After all, mothers are something we were supposed to outgrow.

In her book, *Braiding Sweetgrass*, Robin Wall Kimmerer contrasts her own daughter's refusal to say the pledge of allegiance at school, with the experience of the Thanksgiving Address of the Onondaga Nation, giving thanks for the provision and abundance of nature. She observes, "You can't listen to the Thanksgiving Address without feeling wealthy. And, while expressing gratitude seems innocent enough, it is a revolutionary idea. In a consumer society, gratitude is a radical proposition."[4]

Our societal makeup from the shopping malls to the meeting halls of our churches—I refuse to unilaterally call them sanctuaries when they are not—depends on dissatisfaction. White American Christianity is rooted in unrestricted capitalism, and this bleeds over into the very structure of the religion. Gratitude, as Kimmerer points out, "doesn't send you out shopping to find satisfaction; it comes as a gift rather than a commodity, subverting the foundation of the whole economy."[5] A consumerist society depends on a lack of gratitude. It is an endless yawning chasm of need that seeks to duplicate itself into our very hearts, gorging itself on our manufactured endless want for material symbols as vacuous as the flag we were programmed to revere.

---

[4] Robin Wall Kimmerer, *Braiding Sweetgrass*, 111..
[5] *Ibid.*

Beyond the more obvious issues with this mindset of constant consumption leading to a cycle of constant desire for more and constant waste that damages our home, a lack of gratitude prevents us from understanding that following Jesus was always about an embodied faith. And yet everything from diet culture to faith-healing theology weaponized against those with mental illness, chronic illness, or other disabilities points to a distinct lack of embodiment. Perhaps it's easier to spot as one who resides in a female body, since I was taught to doubt my own body from the start anyway. It was never thin enough. It was inherently sinful because, if I didn't cover it properly, I would lead males in the vicinity into sin.

Once again, a belief inherently lacking in common sense prevails: doesn't this mean men are weak and incapable of controlling themselves which would seem to speak for a lack of ability to lead if they are so led around by their sexual desires that my bathing suit without a baggy t-shirt over it could cause a loss of all self-control? Surely women then should have the power if men are rendered incapacitated by the sight of my shoulders if I'm wearing a spaghetti strap top, or the knowledge that I'm wearing a bra should my straps be in view.

But this mindset is damaging to everyone regardless of the type of body they inhabit. Sure, those who possess strong, healthy, whole, and especially white and male bodies are harmed least by these ideas, but if we look deeper, it is toxic to them as well. This religion of allegiance to consumerism and empty symbols over people and the planet can't help but miss the implications of the incarnation.

***

In Genesis we find back-to-back creation accounts, the first ending with the creation of humans and the second beginning with it. Both accounts single out humanity as unique in creation. In the first, God says "let us make humankind in our image"[6] something that is not said about any other creature. In the second we get a lovely visual and tactile description of God forming the first human by hand and breathing God's own breath into this person's lungs.[7]

---

6 Genesis 1:26 NRSV
7 Genesis 2:7 NRSV

These narratives serve to set humans apart, but not in such a way as to sever the connection with the whole of creation. But the distinction is vital too as here we have the image of God created in flesh or embodied. This act is an incarnation—a little incarnation—that predates, and thus points to, the incarnation when God takes human form in Christ forever creating union between God and humanity. In turn, the incarnation points to the redemption of the world being finalized in the new creation when all separation between creation, humans, and God ceases to exist.

That there was never meant to be any hierarchy at all among humans is evident from this language of creation. Each human is a distinct little incarnation of God intended to participate in the ongoing act of creation in their time and location in history. The creation narrative in Genesis is unique among other ancient Near Eastern narratives about gods and humans. As one commentary explains, "In the ancient Near East the king as image of God was a designated representative of the gods, ruling on their behalf. Genesis 1 Democratizes this royal image so that all humanity belongs to this sphere and the inter-human hierarchical understandings of the image are set aside."[8]

We were made for unity with each other and with God. The lack of trust in God that led to a breaking of the world creates a longing within us to return to the wholeness at the beginning, a wholeness all of Scripture is moving towards, pointing toward the end where everything will be made new; and creation comes full circle.

I've often wondered why God bothers with this. After all, creation is and always will be a messy affair. But I was struck by an earlier line from the same commentary that notes: "The 'let us make' thus implicitly extends to human beings, for they are created in the image of one who chooses to create in a way that shares power with others."[9] God enters the goo of the chrysalis with us, knowing that if we give the process its due, there will be something beautiful on the other side.

In *The Silmarillion,* Tolkien writes an account of creation where his God-character directs the angelic-type beings to sing. Each of these beings understands a piece of the melody—was created with a piece of

---

8 *The New Interpreter's Bible,* 345.
9 *Ibid.*

the melody. It is only when they are directed to combine their music that they begin to understand the whole. One of these beings seeks to draw more power. Instead of singing the music he was created with, he tries to make his own.

This begins to throw the composition off as it confuses some of the beings around him. Some even stop singing as they become "despondent" and lose the thread of the music they were created with. As the discord spreads, the God-character stands and weaves two new threads into the music, bringing even some of the notes from the disruptive strand into the whole, creating a piece that "was deep and wide and beautiful, but slow and blended with an immeasurable sorrow, from which its beauty chiefly came. The other had now achieved a unity of its own; but it was loud and vain, and endlessly repeated. It had little harmony, but rather a clamorous unison as of many trumpets braying upon a few notes. And it essayed to drown the other music by the violence of its voice, but it seemed that its most triumphant notes were taken by the other and woven into its own solemn pattern."[10]

Part of the good news of the gospel isn't that it removes artificial and abusive human hierarchies, it's that they were never supposed to exist. As Lisa Sharon Harper says, "In the person of Jesus, the Kingdom of God had broken into the world. That means the reversal of the Fall is imminent. Creation will be restored."[11] Scripture shows us God's story has always been about God incarnate in history, and that as co-conspirators with God in creation, we each have a distinct role to play in God's ongoing work. This view subverts encounters like the one I related in chapter one where people imposed their expectations on what my song should be, whether through "praying" specific things over me, or creating limits on who and what I could be because I am female. God's sharing of God's own power with humans as core to the act of creation gives us a model to follow that should make us naturally recoil from models where power is consolidated to a few.

The metaphor of the chrysalis breaks down because I feel as though I've been through about three of these periods of questioning and reforming; and, of course, a real butterfly only emerges once.

---
10 J.R.R. Tolkien,.*The Silmarillion*,. 4-5..
11 Lisa Sharon Harper, *The Very Good Gospel*, 113.

But while there's never room to tell the whole story, I discovered that I was beginning to emerge with wings. After the initial round of transformation in seminary, some members of my family and church community at the time weren't comfortable with this transformation. After all, with wings I could fly off anywhere: I was no longer "stable." So they tried their best to convince me I was still a caterpillar. But the thing about wings is, once you've tried them, it's really hard to go back to crawling around on the ground.

It started with the creation accounts in Genesis, and it has continued as an ongoing work of creation: bringing life to every corner of my life. As I discarded various pieces of toxic theology that had been presented to me as essential, the old voices rose up and asked who did I think I was to be making these decisions. As chronic illness put weight on my body, the old voices rose up and told me I was now less worthy than when I was thin. But the seeds of creation will sprout if space is made for them, and the older I get the more I'm learning to fly free of all the voices that seek to make me believe I am a caterpillar.

The fall broke creation specifically because it broke relationships. Right relationship with God, each other, ourselves, and the planet became marred. Going back to Harper, "It wasn't supposed to be this way. The earth is cursed because of humanity's lack of trust in God. Because we chose our own peace above the peace of all, creation suffers."[12] The breaking of these relationships made space for power grabs and subjugation of many people. The fall is a return to the void that existed before God began to speak the world into existence. Accepting God's story is allowing the work of creation to take root in each of us individually and communally. Accepting our role as little incarnations gives us strength to speak life into the voids and to begin to restore pieces of creation into right relationships.

---

12 *Ibid*, 107.

CHRYSALIS

*they told me i was judas
betraying jesus
with all my questions
and doubt
trading Christ in
for the currency of
popularity
because true women of god
never seek pulpits
over potlucks
but they didn't realize
they were the ones
crucifying anything that
threatened their
position
and power
defining righteousness
by the length of each nail
hammered into the hands and feet
of the sinners and rebellious
they claimed to weep at the
foot of the cross
but we know who really showed up
a mother
a sister
a disciple
all loyal women
to a gentle king
and their taunting
no longer bothers me
because i know
my true name
is not judas
but mary
and i am here
to preach
the resurrection
like it
or not*

–Kaitlin Shetler

3

Judas

He leaned towards me across the tiny Starbucks table. "It almost sounds like you're saying you're a..." and here his voice dropped so as not to be overheard, "a feminist." As though this was the ultimate "f" word that couldn't be overheard in polite conversation amidst the murmur of the coffee shop around us. I looked at my friend and just said, "well, yes." And he stared back at me—shocked—as if I'd just denounced my faith. And to him I probably had. He'd been raised like I had: you couldn't be a feminist or a Democrat and be a Christian. All these rigid lines around what Christianity could and couldn't be, as though the gospel needed our protection to keep it from corruption. But who did this protected, rigid gospel benefit? It certainly wasn't the least of these. And it certainly didn't protect me.

This type of Christianity told me I had a specific role and place and to be godly was to stay within those boundaries and also not to question them. After all, you can't have faith if you have doubts right? Thomas was sneered at as a bad example. You shouldn't have had to touch Jesus to believe that Jesus was alive. Thomas, of course, was just the scape-goat to deflect our attention from the fact that it was the men who were hiding behind locked doors. All of them, not just Thomas. Their fear of consequences because of guilt-by-association had them trembling in the dark. The women risked association because their love was greater than their fear. They'd seen what this empire did to their teacher, surely there was some risk involved in going to his tomb. After all, there were soldiers posted to prevent someone from stealing the body. They could have easily been suspects.

Inward Apocalypse: Uncovering a Faith for the Common Good

***

I was probably nine or ten when I encountered the story of Deborah leading the nation of Israel. I don't remember how. I was a precocious reader so perhaps I'd read it myself at that point, I'm not really sure. I asked my dad something about the story. Surely this is "biblical" proof that women can be in church leadership. Surely. "No, no," he said. It was proof of God's deep judgment on Israel. They had "done what was evil" and they were being punished because none of the men would step up, evidenced by Barak not going into battle without Deborah and Jael getting to strike the winning blow by assassinating the enemy general.

One chapter in Judges that contains brief, tiny stories of these two fierce women, and he kicked the legs of their stories out from under me as I tried to hold their power up. Women in leadership are part of God's judgment for men not taking their "god-given" place.

I've got the word "biblical" in quotes because in American Christianity it is probably one of the most abused words there is. Just about anything can be "biblical" if you pull out a tiny portion of the text. The funny thing is in American Christianity certain things have been deemed as contextual and certain things are held as absolute truths. Like a "godly" marriage can only be between a man and a woman and the man is the head of the house.

Incidentally, if we jump back to my early twenties and that conversation with a friend in Starbucks, the argument I'd made that got me called a feminist in those hushed and disapproving tones, was that marriage should be a partnership. Shocking, I know. I hadn't even gotten onto the idea of women in church leadership. Women as bishops. Women as presidents. And we were talking about heterosexual marriage. This was very introductory level stuff here, the idea of marriage as a partnership, but even that was enough to bring out the word "feminist" as though just the invocation of this dirty word would be enough to get me to reexamine what I'd just said.

I chafed against the straight-jacket that this Christianity—this rigid "gospel"—tried to place on me and all of my siblings who had questions or doubts or thought that maybe this wasn't really the freedom Christ had come to offer. How is the subjugation of everyone who isn't a cisgendered, straight, abled, white man good news? If this was the gospel, then the crucifixion was a waste. Just one more brown, indigenous activist killed at the hands of the state whose death was interpreted by those in power to fit their agendas, and it didn't really hold any meaning for the rest of us.

My faith had become to feel like a tapestry whose bindings had been cut and the more threads I pulled, the more it came apart and the more I wondered if there was going to be anything to put back together.

In *Dance of the Dissident Daughter*, Sue Monk Kidd wrestles with some of these questions. On a walk one winter day she reflects, "Mostly, I didn't want to believe that I had been wounded by my own faith. I didn't want to acknowledge how it had regulated half the human population to secondary status and invisible places. I didn't want any of this to be true."[1]

Earlier this week as I wrote this chapter, I had a conversation with an old friend and as we were swapping book recommendations, we discovered we had each made a rule against reading any white, male theologians. We had both attended the same seminary albeit a few years apart as Rachel was in the high-school youth group at the church I worked at in LA. And it wasn't that we hadn't learned a great deal from white male theologians, it's just that they made up at least 90% (and that's probably a generous estimate) of the writers and professors we'd each experienced. In my time at Fuller, I had one Black male professor for one New Testament class, three white female professors, and one Korean female professor. I took one class from each of them so that was five classes out of thirty or so that were necessary to complete my degree.

Feminist theology and liberation theology were both considered to be specialist areas, as opposed to integrated into the whole. I'd never even heard of womanist or mujerista theology, and I only remember a single conversation about queer Christians. None of my classmates were out, and I hadn't come far enough along in my own journey to even realize how strange that was.

What happens when white and male and straight and abled is the default theology and anything else is a specialized class? In thinking

---

[1] Sue Monk Kidd, *The Dance of the Dissident Daughter*, 42..

about divergent experiences, Elizabeth Johnson writes, "Feminist reflection is therefore not alone in its use of human experience as a resource for theology. What is distinctive, however, is its specific identification of the lived experience of women, long derided or neglected in androcentric tradition, as an essential element in the theological task."[2] When you only describe human experience from a single, narrow segment of the population, you not only leave out a lot of people, you also create a theology and a reading of the gospel that is decidedly lacking in multiple dimensions.

In my own life, just the title of Johnson's book, *She Who Is*, was like a drink of fresh, cool water on a hot and thirsty day. *She* who is. Something inside me unclenched as I realized that I had been made fully in the image of Mother God, and that female pronouns for her were just as legit as the male ones. This fits in well with some lovely mother images of God that we find in Scripture to counterbalance just a bit all the heavy male pronouns and father images we see.

Mother God was one thread I could pick up out of the tangle of my faith tapestry lying at my feet and put back on the loom as I tried to envision just what a faith that included all of these humans I had grown to love would look like. Because if it left any of them out, I didn't think I could believe it anymore.

***

For a while in my twenties while I was going to seminary and working at a church, I didn't know anyone who didn't call themselves a Christian. Still hovering on the edge of the evangelical tradition where evangelism—defined internally as sharing the "gospel" with those who are "unsaved"—was an important thing, I was failing completely in my task to do so as I didn't know anyone who I could "share" with. As the pastor of the church I was working for took a deep dive into fundamentalism, he invited a group to come teach us how to share the four spiritual laws (so simple! There's only four!) as an evangelistic tool to assault total strangers at the mall. I was caught between my internal voice screaming "no" and the fact that this was my employer at the time.

---
2 Elizabeth A. Johnson, *She Who Is*, 61.

We had a practice session at the house of one of the kids in my youth group and I was volunteered to play the role of the "unsaved" person in a role play. Even in that scenario I felt how manipulative the whole thing was. I pulled out my best "spiritual, but not religious, agnostic-ish, there's not absolute truth" type character and refused to let the visiting guy convert me. But later at the mall, I felt like I had to be a good example. I was sitting in the food court, and this woman was sitting nearby looking sad. I struck up a conversation about what was going on in her life, and she gratefully shared pieces of her story. I don't remember the specifics. What's stuck in my mind is the moment I tried to do what I was "supposed to" and turn the conversation to how Jesus could solve all her problems. She stiffened visibly, and ended the conversation abruptly. I went back feeling ashamed of myself. I had known it was manipulative, and yet I hadn't listened to my own internal voice. Instead I had shoved it down, and now I had added an injury to this woman who was already having a bad week.

Glennon Doyle talks about finding your own "knowing" in her book, *Untamed*. It's the idea of learning to trust yourself and your instincts, but I didn't know how at that point in my life because I'd been taught the exact opposite. Pre-seminary, I'd absorbed an awful lot of "the heart is deceitfully wicked" type of teaching, and had imbibed this idea that I should doubt myself above all. Especially as a woman. I had yet to parse the fact that the men around me doubted themselves far less than the women did. That woman in the courtyard of my church talking about needing her husband to reign her in had stuck in my head, but I hadn't let my knowing unpack why that rightly had bothered me.

It is something that is overlaid in so many little and big ways. When only one kind of person is allowed to stand up in front and say "this is my body" as they pass out communion and salvation carefully packaged in little plastic cups, it shrinks and diminishes the image of God in everyone else. We were all created in God's image, except that image is better and more fully expressed in the white, straight, cisgendered, abled man. And while this was never explicitly said in anything I ever heard, it was reinforced in so many ways. The head pastors all fit this category. Women and non-white people were associates or lay leaders or children's pastors. Only the men could lead everyone. Disabled people were prayer requests or mascots. Gay people were welcome if they weren't partnered and were appropriately ashamed of themselves. Actually, that was a step up from the church I attended in high school where homosexuality was looked at as something to be cured by God. The only person I knew who identified as such did so as part of his conversion story. He said he had been gay, then he got saved, and God had "healed" him. I'd love to know what happened to him after that. He was dating a girl at the time when he shared his testimony, but in the super rigid purity culture of that church, it probably wasn't that difficult for him to do. It stuck in my memory and later has been unpacked as just one more way that people who don't fit into those rigid definitions that had been drawn by those saying they had the right to lead the church tried to pour themselves into those tiny plastic cups,: desperate for a sip of grace and hearing that the only way they could have any is if they fit inside the mold.

In the introduction to his book, *Does Jesus Really Love Me?*, Jeff Chu tells a story about the disappearance of one of his teachers at the Christian school he attended. Later, the principal told them all the teacher had been dismissed because it was discovered he was in a homosexual relationship. Jeff goes on, "What I remember is that fear swamped me. My palms still get tropical when I think of that chapel. At the mention of the word *homosexual*, I knew the truth. Even if I didn't have words to define it then, I knew I had feelings like Mr. Byer's. And this was the lesson that I learned: Nobody could ever, ever find out, because if they did, I would be damned and cast out, just like he was."[3]

I imagine that this was the point where Jeff's heart broke. Teresa Mateus in her book *Healing Sacred Wounds* describes a conversation where she was told she couldn't be a Christian if she didn't believe that Gandhi would go to hell because he'd never "professed Jesus." "This was the moment," she says, "This was the moment my heart broke. I had never even considered that there were qualifying factors to my goodness and Godness; I didn't know there was fine print that was non-negotiable. I wasn't even sure I believed the ultimatum but just

---

[3] Jeff Chu, *Does Jesus Really Love Me?* 4.

a shred of that possibility, that I could not really be Christian slipped into my consciousness and could not be unwritten."[4]

The more conversations I have with people—people who've left evangelical churches, people who no longer call themselves Christians, people who no longer know where they fit—there is the sense that each person has had this moment where they've come up against one or more things they've been told they absolutely must believe or they cannot be a Christian, and they turn away sadly because they've been given an ultimatum they must refuse for their sake of their own humanity.

This turning away is not like the turning away of the rich young man in Matthew where he let his possessions come between him and eternal life, but rather, these people turn away because they've been told to affirm or deny something so toxic, so rigid, that if they have to believe that to be a Christian, it's their faith that has to go.

If you believe that women can be pastors and preach, then you can't be a Christian. If you believe that you can be a faithful Christian and be queer, then you actually can't be a Christian. If you vote Democrat, then you can't be a Christian. If you believe in taking care of the environment, you're putting other things above Christ. If. If. If. Like the moment when that woman ended the conversation with me in the food court that day, my inner voice tried to tell me that all of this was likewise manipulative. That these beliefs existed to consolidate power to a few. That none of this had anything to do with loving people like Jesus loved people.

All the "ifs" contort the definition of Christian until it has both expanded beyond someone trying to follow Christ by the addition of so many at the very least non-essential and at the worst harmful things the striving Christian must adhere to, and has also contracted to a narrowly fenced and rigid set of beliefs that leave the majority of people out in the cold. "Jesus died for the whole world," they preach, and in the next breath condemn the world to hellfire and damnation. "Roman Catholics aren't real Christians," they preach, because they've traded freedom in Christ for rules and idols, and then they turn around and impose the very burden they claim to lift. Only they trade historical connection and icons for the idols of nationalism, conservatism, and

---
4 Teresa B. Pasquale, *Sacred Wounds*, 16

white supremacy—each more dangerous than the supposed "Mary-worship" they abhor without understanding. "There's freedom in Christ," they preach, while strapping heavy burdens to the backs of those who come to the cross, in some sort of a reverse parody of John Bunyan's imagery of the Christian with his burden of sin that rolled away at the cross.

They thus turn Christ into the kind of God that needs to be carried around and defended, a God like the gods the prophet in Isaiah was decrying in chapter 46 as needing to be carried around literally, the heavy idols imposing a burden on the people as they were exiled, sapping the energy of the people in an already trying time. "If energy is what is in short supply," writes Walter Brueggemann, "it is better to find a God who is free, able, and willing to take responsibility for his godness."[5]

***

The other day I shared a meme on Facebook that read, "Have you considered: People deserve food, shelter, and medicine whether or not they can produce profitable labor." This sparked a multi-commented debate from certain people who identified as Christians about how the church was somehow supposed to do this for all of society. This of course is a red herring. It took me a long time to realize this, but being raised in churches and circles where this was the accepted viewpoint of the majority, I was taught to believe that somehow shifting this responsibility to the government was wrong. Of course it's nonsensical in a pluralistic society to have one religion responsible for the needs of the poor, especially when it is far more effective to put in place government policies—ones far more rigorous than even what we currently have—that aim to give people a good quality of life and dignity.

Somehow this isn't a "Christian" worldview coming from the tradition I was raised in. And lest I make it sound as though this is only endemic in certain evangelical or charismatic denominations and non-denominational churches, both people who chimed in actually attend, or at least attended in the past, an Episcopal church.

---
5 Walter Brueggemann, *Prophetic Imagination*, 73..

This goes back to why I and others refer to these mindsets as white American Christianity: 1) they transcend many church labels and take root in a variety of places and 2) there are aspects to this brand of fundamentalism that are unique to majority white churches in the United States.

Arguing that perhaps it is "Christian" after all to work towards a government that will provide opportunities for all of its citizens to thrive has gotten me the same censure, shocked tones, and baleful glances I received that day in the cafe from my friend who could barely get the word "feminist" out for fear of being overheard saying something indecent in public. And then out comes the red herring. Because most of the people who argue it's the church that should care for the poor are doing almost nothing to care for the poor. Like Judas taking issue with Mary's sacrificial and prophetic anointing of Jesus' feet in the gospel of John[6], the poor are often just an excuse, a means to an end, a distraction to wave in front of people's faces as part of the true mission of the church, and then discarded when no longer valuable to the argument.

Arguing that it is only the church's role to care for the poor comes wrapped in the argument that the church is somehow better equipped to "get people back on their feet" as one commenter argued on my post "so they can provide for themselves and not [create] a lifestyle of dependency." Which again is a false argument because as studies[7] have shown where communities have run experiments with a universal basic income, overall employment goes up, not down, and the ripple effects of stress reduction reach the wider community. People want to have meaningful work as it contributes to satisfaction and dignity.

Of course the argument in my post was about people who can't work full-time: people with mental illness, chronic illness, or other disabilities that prevent the nine-to-five grind from working for them personally. And somehow arguing that these people—including me— deserve some level of basic care is contributing to the fabled "lifestyle of dependency." Because for all the surface language about being saved by grace, there's a deep undercurrent of merit-based beliefs around how much faith a person has. This faith is measurable by one's relative

---
6 John 12:1-8 NRSV
7 Rachel Treisman, "California Program Giving $500 No-Strings-Attached Stipends Pays Off, Study Finds." .

health and wealth. If you have enough faith, you'd be "healed." If you have enough faith, and you work hard enough, you wouldn't be poor. These beliefs ignore the realities of the supremacies of our systems and put the blame for people's place in society on the individuals themselves. This means that the individuals most vulnerable and in need of social safety nets find themselves helped the least. But that's okay, because it's their fault, right?

All of this comes not from a Christianity based in the arcs of justice and shalom we see through the Scripture and life of Christ, but from a veneer of religiosity that has both evolved and been crafted to allow certain people to remain in power. Rather than a religion rooted in love, American Christianity has put down roots in supremacy that benefits white, straight, cisgendered, abled males and demands the subjection of everyone else in a twisted mockery of holiness. After all, as bell hooks writes, "Domination cannot exist in any social situation where a love ethic prevails. Jung's insight, that if the will to power is paramount love will be lacking, is important to remember." This juxtaposition is telling. The lack of a love ethic among those who call themselves Christians reveals the will to power as the dominant god in this twisting of the Christian faith. hooks continues, "When love is present the desire to dominate and exercise power cannot rule the day."[8]

This pervasive belief system masquerading as Christianity has crept into various traditions and flavors of the church preaching a message of power and supremacy that allows its adherents to create a hierarchy of holiness and shift responsibility for those at the bottom of their hierarchy to the individuals themselves. This message could not be further from the gospel.

**

So as I unpacked and examined various aspects of my faith, I was met with increasing amounts of push back. I remember arguing for the acceptance of Syrian refugees and the person I was talking to responded with a verbal pat on the head, "Oh, you just want to love everyone." This was after they'd argued the refugee crisis was an

---
8 bell hooks, *All About Love*, 98.

Islamic plot to sneak terrorists into the country. Once again I found myself perplexed because, yes, loving everyone is exactly what I wanted to do, and I thought that was sort of the whole point to this following Jesus thing.

It felt like every time I circled back around one of these areas, the push-back increased. I was Judas, betraying my faith and community and conforming my mind to the pattern of the world. That was yet another handy little text used to argue that anything originating outside the teachings of this brand of Christianity was somehow antithetical to faith. It didn't matter what it was, or how much more it might have resembled Jesus. I was taught not to look for what God was doing in the world, because such an idea was not even considered, but rather to use this faith as a bludgeon to defend against the attacks of a world that was always in opposition to the true believer.

"We restore and reclaim things from the grip of hate the best way we know how, not because it is ours to restore out of a sense of ownership, but because the work of love is never finished."
–Kaitlin Curtice, *Native*, p. 74

4

Creation

"What does it matter? It's all going to burn anyway." He leaned back in his chair, a challenge in his eyes. I don't even remember exactly what I'd said that led to this response, but it had something to do with care of the planet, something about conserving our natural resources. I was so flabbergasted in the moment, I didn't even respond, but this has stuck in my head for years following the conversation.

In high school, I had one of those WWJD? bracelets as a symbol of my devotion to be as Christ-like as I could and to ask myself in any given situation, "what would Jesus do?" Perhaps the joke's on them, because as much as the people who participate in the belief system I left behind would decry my current beliefs as having been "infected by social justice," as a writer colleague of mine was recently accused of, I read the gospel. I am pretty confident I was radicalized by Jesus.

See Jesus said this thing I think is key, and in fact is one of the only verses I believe it's safe to quote without a long research project. Most of the Bible has to be understood from the context in which it was written in order to see how God is meeting people where they are and nudging them in the direction of justice and liberation and equality. But this one passage, the one where Jesus is asked, "what is the greatest commandment?" and Jesus responds "Love the Lord your God with all your heart and love your neighbor as yourself, on these two things hang all of scripture," this passage is a key lens to interpreting how we view what Jesus does and what God is doing throughout this story of God's relationships with humans. Now reading it as "on this hangs all of scripture" is my paraphrase. The text actually says, "on this hangs all the law and the prophets." This is a shorthand for all of scripture written in that day, however, as what was then scripture would be what we now call the Hebrew Bible, which was largely adapted into what we call the Old Testament of the Christian Bible. And that set of scriptures is called the Tanakh, which is an acronym for the law (Torah), the prophets (Nevi'im), and the writings (Ketuvim). So when Jesus says, "on this hangs all the law and the prophets," he's saying "on this hangs all of scripture" and I think it's safe to say on that hangs all of the scripture that was written after his sojourn among us.[1]

So then returning to my now ex-friend's bombastic declaration about "it's all gonna burn." Not for nothing, this person and his wife are some of the people who have unfriended me on Facebook and fallen out of my life. We'd met during a season of working with him on a ecumenical youth ministry project for our region. But after I started going public with my more "progressive" viewpoints over the last eight or nine years, particularly after the 2016 election, they were some of the people I found were no longer listed as friends. While I can't be certain, most of the people that abruptly vanished from my timelines and conversations around that time were people who call themselves Christians and yet managed to vote for a decidedly un-Christlike candidate. Supporting a president who worked actively to reverse many environmental protections fits in with this "it's all gonna burn" mentality, and while it has far reaching implications for our planet, this mentality is actually a core mentality that leads to abuse of, well, everything, not just the planet.

***

As a youth minister, I was underpaid in every vocational church job I worked at. Whether stated or not, the idea I was working for God and therefore should be willing to sacrifice is something that is at the core of many pay structures within our organizations. Building in rest and time off was something that happened better with the Episcopal church than in the more evangelical world, but all too often exhaustion was still a badge of honor because the work of God is so important that we must never really stop. After all, we can rest when we're dead.

---
[1] See "Poisoned Bible Project 1: Does God Hate Women?"

This of course is imported from American capitalism, or maybe American capitalism based it on that infamous puritan work ethic, I'm not sure. But in this toxic chicken-and-egg scenario, where it came from doesn't matter so much as how it affects literally everything. The idea that everything from the gift of creation to human lives can be reduced to some kind of monetary value is a perverted twisting of the abundance of God's intent for human thriving. But if this world and the precious humans who live on its surface are to be treated as disposable, what is that building towards? I find it hard to believe that one can hold such a belief and then think they can get to the new earth and flip a switch to participating in conservation and justice. What do they believe about the new earth? Is it a pleasure planet to be trashed relentlessly only now God magically restores it at intervals? And how would that be heaven? And if the poor don't matter here because they will "get their reward" later, what reward waits for those who refused to help them in this world? And what would Jesus say about that?

That's actually an easy one because we have a literal story Jesus told about that as a warning to those who refuse to help the poor. In Luke, we find the story of the rich man and Lazarus. In the parable, the unnamed rich man passes by Lazarus every time he goes in or out of his house, and yet does nothing to ease his affliction, not even giving him leftovers from his tables or ointment for his sores. So then when they both die, a dramatic image is painted of Lazarus being comforted and the rich man living in agony. The rich man begs for help--get this--from Lazarus, first to give him some water, then to go back to his house and warn his brothers. And Abraham's wonderfully dry response is that they had scripture and if they ignored what scripture had to say about the right treatment of the poor, then someone rising from the dead isn't going to convince them.

Yet somehow this story doesn't seem to pervade the what-would-Jesus-do culture of helping the poor. While this culture is big on mission trips to those "other" places when it looks good on Instagram feeds, its participants often actively fight against systems that would prevent poverty and promote human thriving. And imperfect as they might be, how would systems that lift people out of poverty not be at least somewhat oriented towards God's kingdom? While we can't achieve the perfections of the new earth yet, we can move towards those goals. If all will be made new and right and just and equitable in the new earth, should we not assume those are goals to be valued by those of us who claim to follow God? It doesn't make sense to me to relegate all of that to only the hereafter and not work towards that in the here-and-now. Are we not called to participate in making all things new?

All too often when I look at white evangelical American Christianity, somehow "all things new" has been reduced to internal, individual lives. The idea that the only thing that matters is the "salvation of souls," as if souls exist on their own and nothing else matters. This unholy bifurcation of beings creates a perfect mechanism for the folks following this vaguely Christian-esque philosophy to actively participate in all manner of un-Christ-like oppressive systems and claim none of that matters because it's only souls God cares about.

Like the worst of hikers who leave their trash on the trail, this group of "world is not my home, I'm just a-passin' through" folks treat the planet and its residents as equally disposable in a blasphemous contortion of hand-picked pericopes used as shields to deflect anything else from Scripture that might challenge them to rethink the systems of oppression they actively prop up. And like Abraham in the parable, I'm also convinced that someone returning from the dead would have no affect on their beliefs. After all, Jesus already did, and they knit his resurrection into their own toxic theologies instead of seeing the ultimate sign act that should have had them following Jesus' disruption of oppression everywhere. What would Jesus do indeed.

To me, it seems obvious how short a jump it is from the destruction of the planet via endless commodification to the commodification of almost all people. After all, this isn't new. Using people as disposable resources is a story as old as humans themselves. The only lives that have ever really mattered are those of the rich and powerful. American capitalism meeting the invention of white supremacy just put a different sort of spin on it. If we meld the myth of the American dream into white supremacy there's the idea that anyone—well, any white person anyway—can work hard and become one of those rich, powerful people. You know, the ones that really matter. This is the only explanation I can think of—and I'm not alone in this, I've seen it floating around discussions for several years—why regular people keep voting against wealth taxes and other things. They don't think of themselves as middle or working class folks. They see themselves as future rich people.

As one Guardian article noted in 2012:

> "Americans are particularly reluctant to describe themselves as even working class let alone poor. A Pew survey in 2008 revealed that 91% believe they are either middle class, upper-middle class or lower-middle class. Relatively few claim to be lower class or upper class, intimating more of a cultural aspiration than an economic relationship."[2]

What does it mean for society that those who amass vast resources and very rarely use those to any large extent to benefit those with fewer resources are held up on so high a pedestal? Instead of trying to make a society where everyone can thrive, we continue to perpetuate a society where only a few can truly thrive. How is it that the ultra-rich are seen as paragons of virtue instead of parasites who leech money out of the lifeblood of the average worker, converting their sweat into wealth for themselves and only redistributing a pittance too small to really live on for those doing all the actual labor?

This is where the myth of the American Dream comes into play. The myth itself has been commodified as a powerful tool in the hands of the ultra-rich. Almost all of them have some sort of bootstrap story that goes like this: they had little, they worked hard, now they are rich. The bootstrap myth is a powerful piece of the overall American Dream myth, and one that completely overlooks the structures of power and supremacy in our system. Almost all of the ultra rich bootstrappers are white men, a huge double advantage that has been programmed into the DNA of our country from the beginning. Most of them weren't truly poor when they started out, but built what they did on the backs of their immigrant families who eked out an existence for their families and parents and grandparents who worked themselves to the bone to provide education and benefits for their children. So even if these men

---
2 Gary Younge "Working Class Voters: Why America's Poor are Willing to Vote Republican"

came from poverty, it was often several generations before, and their personal stories ignore the several-generational arc that helped them launch.

The next piece is that none of these men achieve wealth alone. Even if they did invent a product, they need labor to produce and distribute it, and choosing to keep that labor barely paid so they can reap more of the benefits for themselves is an evil choice that people seem to overlook. The workers deserve a living wage period. The reasons people work for less than living wages—and I am defining this as more than survival but room to actually live and thrive—is that our society is lock-step against creating better wages for people.

I'm not an economist, so I can't get into the nitty-gritty of why things like trickle-down economics are completely misleading. I can just look at the amount of money in the world and say, there is no shortage of resources. Everyone could be thriving together, only we continue to prop up systems based on completely false ideas of people needing to earn or deserve certain measures as though the "poor" are all lazy and poor through their own fault.

I have several friends who have fallen below and then climbed back above the poverty line, and one thing that sticks out from their stories is the amount of work it takes to be poor. Some of them only climbed out again due to family aid: say being able to move back into a parent's house for a while to get back on their feet. But what happens when no such resources are available?

Not fighting for a basic level of thriving for everyone means we believe some people are more worthy than others, that some people don't deserve comfort, that they don't deserve rest, that they are less-than. Less than what? Fully human, I guess.

When we circle back to the so-called "puritan work ethic" we see a different spin on this, one we religious types all too often inflict on ourselves. Here in white, American evangelicalism anyway there is a subculture that purports to thrive on too little money and exhaustion, wearing both as badges of honor that proclaim how little the "things of this world" matter. In this toxic stew, we commodified ourselves, devalued our work, our bodies' needs, and our very lives, rushing through this sin-swept plain, elevating ourselves above the base worldliness of our culture, and anticipating nothing more than our own deaths where we would finally be rewarded.

We set examples of self-commodification that we expected others to follow and if they didn't, we helped impose that on them. After all, we were leading by example. We were also consuming our own lives as though they were disposable. As though we were disposable. And that's not really living. It took being sick for a bunch of years in a row—a sickness caused by a genetic predisposition triggered by stress and chronic trauma—to finally be able to accept myself as intrinsically worthy. Not what I did, nor what I had accomplished, nor what I could produce, but just me, just existing. And if I discounted my own worth for so many years, holding my resume up as a thin shield against the forces that would seek to declare me unworthy, what was I thinking automatically about the worth of others? And what kind of life was I leading, rushing forward at this pace, seeking to accumulate accolades and acclaim, adding sentences and paragraphs to my resume? "See!" It shouted at the world, "Anna has done all these things and is worthy of existence!" But what was I missing?

This type of life lived as a mad rush to the end seems to be opposite of the values of the new creation and the new earth. If Jesus' work on the cross was to make all things new, and we are called to participate in his work, all things implies a vast deal more than simply the "salvation" of souls. If the whole body and whole life matters, then it stands to reason that our neighborhoods matter, our cities and the way they are run matter, the government of the nation matters, and how we treat the planet ultimately matters as well.

***

I paced my porch, mind wandering, but present enough to watch how I put my weight on my left ankle. Inexplicably on a short, mostly flat hike the day before, a tendon in my ankle started burning. I'd wrapped it in an ace bandage, and was pacing my front porch instead of walking anywhere else because it's level and put less pressure on the tendon. As my foot warmed up, the pain subsided, plus I fed it hikers' " vitamin i" (ibuprofen) before I started my restless pacing routine. The fact that I was pacing my porch on a sore tendon probably tells you something about me. I couldn't quit and rest because I was on day thirty of a thirty day streak trying to get ten thousand steps a day, or about four miles of distance. And while I think you should be able to miss a day and have it not reset you to zero, that's not how it works, so I was determined to achieve my little badge in my phone app, this tiny thing made of pixels and no substance. I broke it into sections and elevated my foot in between, reading a book for research, alternating between restless motion of my mind and my legs. I paused at the end of the railing to examine the blossoms on the bush at the end of my porch. This was a tiny bush twelve years ago when we moved into this house and now it wraps itself around the corner of my porch, waving gently above my head even though my porch is a full six feet off the ground and I stand over five and a half feet above that.

It was getting ready to flower, and I examined the branches closest to me trying to guess which blossoms would pop open first. I'd watched the slow progression of buds forming as everything has slowed down in the spring of 2021. You might think the spring of 2020 was when time stopped as the pandemic lockdowns began, and in a way it did, but in other ways the days rolled together in non-stop uniformity, rolling up time and dragging us all along with it until it was somewhere in the middle of summer and school was about to start again. I remember the first few days of the lockdown, and then nothing until September really.

But somewhere between the endless monotony and the uncertainty, I started hiking again. Somehow it doesn't cause my chronic illnesses to flare, and the stronger I get the more the flares have minimized. I feel like I've discovered some sort of magic cure, only I know there's no such thing and I have no idea if it will last, but the hiking seems to be making everything better and now I'm terrified to stop. This imbues my trip planning with a sort of manic energy at times, and I feel like I'm dragging my husband along some days even though he was the one who initiated all this in the first place. He'd had a dream of hiking the Appalachian Trail, section hiking it, given that it would be hard to take off the required amount of time to thru-hike it. And so we talked about what it would take to get in shape to do that, and I bought some trail runners and read my first thru-hike story.

Creation

I guess you could say I got trail fever, but I discovered hiking quiets the exhausting, ongoing noise in my brain. Sometimes the harder the trail, the more quiet that's produced. Time zooms in and there's nothing but the next step up the hill, and no way to get where I'm going except to keep putting one foot in front of the other. "Tired feet, quiet mind:" I saw that phrase on a t-shirt someone posted and it has definitely been my experience. Time slows to an almost observable pace and moments become crystal-clear memories shining bright in my mind.

Before I saw flowers blooming in the woods as I raced by in my car. Spring ephemerals, they're called, a whole class of flowers known for the fleeting amount of time they bloom. Only when I started going out into the woods several times a week and watching the process, I discovered they are around longer than I ever realized, with more variety and variation, and there's really a couple of waves of them, and there are flowers that only bloom in the secret understory of the forest. They all were waiting to introduce themselves to me, waiting for me to slow down enough to hear their brief small voices singing above the leaf litter, only loud enough to be heard if you stop right beside them.

What else have I been missing? As much as I try to resist it, the siren call of modern life seeks to drag us into ever-faster motion as if the motion itself has purpose. Don't slow down, don't think, don't engage, just move from one thing to the next thing, and the only exit is death. After all, that's when you get to rest. But living like that means you miss, well, your life among many other important things along the way.

There's reasons that time blurs together, trauma being a big one that I've experienced both on an individual level from my past, and later on a collective level with the pandemic.

The name of this book has an intentional double meaning. We tend to think of apocalypse as the end of the world, but it also means a revelation or an uncovering. The pandemic was an apocalypse by that definition and a global one at that. Post-apocalyptic fiction usually entails a much darker scenario, not one where many of us managed to keep our houses, though not all of us. Most of us survived, though many of us were lost along the way. The end of one world presented us with opportunities to see the cracks in society and to change what we are doing. It was a revelation, if we are willing to see it and act on its lessons before the next one. See I don't think the world ends just once: it dies and is reborn much as our lives end and begin again. We have survived and moved through things we thought would be the end of us personally or collectively.

Each time we come through an apocalypse and rebuild, we are emulating the new creation that is to come for all of time. Practice rebirth. Embrace the rebuilding. I'm not trying to glorify pain, suffering, abuse, or trauma, just the growth on the other side.

***

I sat very still in a reclining chair, the smooth leather pressing up against me as I reminded myself to relax. The buzz of the tattoo machine provided constant background noise to the awkward small talk. I'd chosen a new artist for this tattoo as my first one was more spur of the moment and simpler, so while it came out okay, it didn't require the research and planning of my second. I'd made the mistake of inviting an acquaintance along with me. She wanted to get a tattoo she'd said, and I thought coming would provide her the information she needed to not be nervous about it. Instead she rattled on about what it looked like to have tattoos and what it meant as a mom etc. Yes, in a tattoo shop surrounded by either tattoo artists or clients, talking to me who was getting one and the artist who was as most tattoo artists are sporting full sleeves and more.

Her chatter was an ironic backdrop to the meaning of my tattoo. I was getting a black-and-gray Sitka spruce on the inside of my right forearm. I wanted it to symbolize embracing my past so I could take charge of writing the rest of my story. My youngest was just over a year old at the time, and I wanted to take charge of my past trauma so that it could no longer run me. Of course this is an ongoing process, not a one time thing.

I'd wanted the tattoo to mean this, and I wanted a redwood-style tree, but I wasn't sure why these two things seemed to go together. As I was browsing Pinterest yet again to add more ideas to my board, I saw one person had a Sitka spruce on their arm. A Sitka spruce! The

Creation

proverbial light bulb started flashing above my head. Sitka. Alaska. I quickly googled the place of my birth. Not only is the sitka spruce the state tree of Alaska, but when I pulled up the address of the house where I was born, I was able to get a street view on Google maps and it was surrounded by Sitka spruces. From that moment on, I couldn't get the ink on my arm fast enough. When we write our own stories, take the helm of our own lives, we are participating in making all things new. We are fully engaging in our role in the new creation.

***

In the beginning God created. And God looked at their creation and called it "good." I sort of picture God leaning back on that seventh day, beer in hand, admiring a job well-done. As I noted in chapter 2, there are two creation stories in the book of Genesis. Realizing this in seminary was a crucial piece to setting me on a path to freedom from fundamentalism, but it's also so much more than that. There are two stories, two myths, and while the fundamental teaching of them is the same, the things don't happen in the same order. This frees us from an overly literal application and lets us ask what is the lesson we are supposed to be learning here.

In *Native,* Kaitlin B. Curtice looks at the overlapping themes in indigenous creation stories and the creation stories in scripture. She concludes:

> "As I learn more about my own story, I am realizing that the bloodline of God is connected to *everything*, no matter how it was first created in the beginning. The shells on the ocean shore, the mushrooms growing in the forest, the trees stretching to the clouds, the tiniest speck of snow in the winter, and *our dust-to-dustness*—we are all connected and tethered to this sacred gift of creation."[3]

In both creation myths in Genesis, God creates, establishing their identity right at the beginning as Creator. Humans are created and

---
[3] Kaitlin Curtice, *Native,* 20-21.

invited to help in the care-taking of the planet. What follows is the establishment of a series of relationships: between God and creation, God and humans, humans and creation, and finally humans with each other. None of these relationships are complete without the other. We can't claim to be in good relationship with God if we mistreat people. We can't claim to be in good relationship with God if we mistreat the planet. We can't claim to be in good relationships with each other if we mistreat the planet. All of these relationships must be moving toward full conciliation if we are to say we are following in the footsteps of Creator God. If we are to participate in making all things new, we must work on making all things new in each of these areas, for the neglect of one is the neglect of all.

In discussing the relationship of God and creation, Elizabeth A. Johnson provides us with this model of mutuality when she states: "Holy Wisdom transcendingly embraces all of finite existence in an inclusive relation that sets it free and calls it to communal, personal, and cosmic shalom."[4] Communal, personal, and cosmic shalom are irrevocably linked. We cannot experience shalom on just one of these levels. Rather, it is only by moving toward shalom and true thriving, justice, and equity for all of us—the rest of creation included—that we can experience it at all.

---

[4] Elizabeth A. Johnson, *She Who Is*, 232.

CREATION

*"Who are the women in your life who have come
before you?
What are their stories?
How did they embody their truth?"*
—Rozella Hadée White, *A Rhythm of Prayer*, p. 126

5

Mother

Standing off the trail, feet spread apart, I finally got over my mental block about peeing outside with my new FUD (female urinary device). I'm elated at this thing that should have been simple finally working. My boys pee outside as naturally as in and I've long been jealous of this. It struck me really this year that of course women have been peeing outside for as long as men—at least until the invention of toilets. And yet it's a topic of major conversation in the all female hiking group I joined on Facebook to get tips, and indeed it was one of my major hangups and obstacles to doing longer trails. I didn't want to be miserable or dehydrated. Somehow we'd been relegated to the indoors for years, with long-distance hikes like the Appalachian Trail long dominated by men—and mostly white men at that. Even now only about one third of thru-hikers and long section hikers on the AT are female.

The next topic that women express the most doubt about is doing things alone. But most—as in pretty much 100%—of the women who have hiked or backpacked alone say they feel safer in the woods than in the city.

My theory is this is more about expectation of women's roles than actual reality. For example, in the fourth Harry Potter movie there's a scene with a formal dance, and Ron is bugging Hermione about who she's going with because in his words a "bloke" can show up on his own and it's fine but for a girl it's "just sad." And somehow there's this idea that men doing stuff on their own if they want to be on their own is normal, but women are either unwanted or being transgressive if they decide to go at something alone.

Back to long-distance hiking for a moment. While many people of any gender don't understand the desire to spend days or weeks at time slowly walking through the woods getting gradually smellier and dirtier, women are subjected to more questions when they announce they are long-distance hiking alone. And yet the desire to explore isn't gendered, it's just human. Hikers are just hikers and it shouldn't matter what other identity markers they have.

I read one female-specific guide to the Appalachian Trail and was put off by the author repeatedly saying how good it was to be "one of the boys." It was sad. She couldn't embrace her femaleness in a male-dominated space, she felt the pinnacle of success was to be seen as a "boy." Ironic especially as she was doing this in her forties and couldn't see her woman-ness as important, it was like on the trail she finally got to shed that. And I get what was driving her comments, but true equality and equity is about being able to be fully you, not adapting to other people's definitions to feel like you fit in. Because I've tried that, and it's miserable.

When I was a kid, I would get impatient waiting for my mom on trips. It seemed to take her forever to get ready to go in the morning while I was up and ready to go as fast as my dad or my brother. I'm not really sure how, but in my head this became a girl-versus-boy sort of thing, and I promised myself I'd never "keep the men waiting." As it turns out, I'm just not that kind of girl, but the kind of girl I am is just as valid as one who wants to spend an hour on her hair. There's actually nothing gendered about that either, my husband has more personal care products than I do. It's literally a personal preference thing. So many things have been assigned categories based on societal expectations around these constructs of gender and have people trimming off the interesting edges of themselves in order to fit the box, not rock the boat, not be singled out as different. I resisted efforts to make me more "girly" as a teenager through young adult, but then I wondered if that was really "me" so I went through a belated couple of phases of trying on different styles and such until I realized that I was right as a kid, I'm just not that "girly" or femme or whatever you want to call it, but that makes me more me, not less. My makeup expired during the pandemic and at this point, I've yet to replace it. If I want to in the future, I will, it's just currently not a priority.

I told a friend of mine I was doing a solo "shakedown" backpacking hike (a shakedown is a trial run, short and close to home so you can fine-tune gear and what you bring before taking on a longer trek). She gave a little gasp and said, "Bring all the things! Like pepper spray! And knife and..." I don't remember the rest of her list. I thought she was joking at first. But after I got that reaction from others as well, I realized they were serious. Bring all things. I don't, for the record, bring all the things. While I have a pocket knife, I don't intend to use it for self-defense. There are no bears in the areas I started out in, and if push comes to shove, I do have actual self-defense training. But I generally feel safer in the woods than the city, and I think the odds of anything happening to me out there are much less than the average danger of driving my car to get there.

Part of people's reactions to me hiking or backpacking solo have to do with their being unfamiliar with the outdoors and the woods at least to the extent of spending several days at a time outside. I get it, the things we are habituated to seem less dangerous. That's why I bring up the danger of driving. It's actually one of the most dangerous things we do on any given day. My odds of dying in a car crash are approximately 1 in over 100.[1] Now this is lifetime odds, meaning that your chances of dying in your lifetime[2] in a car crash are less than 1%. Car crash data varies from year to year, but your odds of dying every time you get in your car are more like 1 in 8,000 or so.[3] By comparison, my odds of being struck by lightning in my life are about 1 in 138,000 at the lowest estimate I've seen.[4] Thus driving is a lot more dangerous than hiking. As far as I can tell, my lifetime odds of dying while hiking are about 1 in 15,000[5] and like the car crash, the odds are lower if one is prepared. Most fatalities are actually day hikers who get lost and weren't hiking with the ten essentials of survival that I carry with me pretty much no matter what hike I'm doing.

---

[1] Between 102 and 107 depending on which source you look at. Here's one New York Times article that puts it at 103 https://www.nytimes.com/2019/01/14/us/opioids-car-crash-guns.html
[2] https://injuryfacts.nsc.org/all-injuries/preventable-death-overview/odds-of-dying/data-details/
[3] https://www.iii.org/fact-statistic/facts-statistics-mortality-risk
[4] Odds of being struck by lightning are cited as high as 1 in 500,000 depending on the source, but here's an insurance table that has them at 1 in 138,000 and was a more reliable source than some of the others I checked https://injuryfacts.nsc.org/all-injuries/preventable-death-overview/odds-of-dying/
[5] Infographic created from several sources including the CDC. All sources linked on this page: https://www.besthealthdegrees.com/health-risks/

When I went to the hospital for my second c-section, I'd been nervous, so I'd looked up the odds of something bad happening because of the surgery. And when I realized that it was many times more dangerous just to drive to the hospital I took a deep breath. A nurse came in before the procedure and handed me a lengthy, scary form to sign. He started to go over it with me and I waved him off. I pointed out that the chances of any of the bad things happening were less than the risk I had taken by driving here that day, and while I understood the hospital needed me to sign it, I didn't really want to hear the litany again. He was surprised and then, dare I say, a tad impressed by my logic.

Since I figured that out about the c-section, I've used the "safer than driving" test for many things. Life is not risk free. So it's better to live the life you want, write the story you want, than to try to get rid of all risk. I think we know this deep down. Risk is also something that's not gendered, it's just part of living in this wild, brutal, beautiful world. My risk of dying in a c-section was less than my risk of dying while driving. And my risk of being struck by lightning while camping is so much smaller than any of those as to be practically non-existent. I mean, you can always be the one, and that would stink. But there's more than 99 chances of not being the one. I'll take those odds. I've got my own story to write, and a few risks is what make the story worth reading.

***

Someone asked me as part of a newsletter series I was doing called the Poisoned Bible Project, why the Bible made it sound like God killed Jesus to save us. This isn't the first time I've heard this interpretation of events on the cross, but what was interesting to me was in the context of the Google form I'd put up for submissions, was the verses this person had cited as problematic. They were the words of institution in Matthew and Luke: "This cup is the new covenant in my blood."

As an Episcopalian, I hear those words every Sunday as we take communion every Sunday. It made me wonder just how hard it would be to go to communion if someone is troubled by these verses. Do they

Mother

even go to communion any more? Do we not do a good enough job of explaining the paschal mystery we celebrate, leaving people to form their own conclusions about something that could very easily seem violent, disturbing, and wrong on so many levels. What kind of parent kills their child intentionally even to save the world? Answer: an evil one. So where does that leave us with God?

The answer–like God–is complex. First of all, if we say we believe in this God we have to understand the concept of this three-in-oneness of the nature of God that cannot adequately ever be described. But suffice it to say the idea that God killed Jesus divides God in essence because Jesus is God even though Jesus also talks about God. So God didn't kill God's son, God gave of Godself.

In her foundational work, *She Who Is*, Elizabeth A. Johnson looks at God–a suffering God–in light of what it means if God is viewed as Mother. She looks at the relationality of women, how women tend to enter into each other's suffering first rather than just trying to save or solve the problem. Now I must interject to say I think this is fundamentally a human thing, but one that has been lost to toxic masculinity, and it would greatly benefit all of us if it could be regained across the genders. In God-on-the-cross, we see a God who enters into human suffering in order to stand on the side of the suffering and oppressed and in so doing, redeem the world. "Especially in situations of massive suffering due to injustice, such a symbol makes clear that God is to be found on the side of those who are oppressed, as a challenge to oppressors be they individuals or structures. The close correlation between divine pathos and prophetic act in the Bible indicates that responsible action for resistance, correction, and healing are among the truest expressions of living faith."[6]

There's an early Christian metaphor-turned-artwork I love that depicts Jesus as a mother pelican. Based on a myth that in times of starvation, a mother pelican would pierce her own breast and feed her chicks from her blood, early Christians saw an analogy here to what Jesus did for us on the cross. Unable to save ourselves or right the world broken by human sin, we needed mom to come in and sort things out for us. And so mom came to earth and saved us with her own blood. Yes, I realize the mom/her pronouns for Jesus are a tad mind-

---

[6] Elizabeth A. Johnson, *She Who Is*, 268.

wrinkling at first, but if we step away from the over-identification with Jesus' gender, then the actions of Jesus in going to the cross make a lot of sense in this metaphor. And as a mom, I identify with this a lot, given the number of times (a day) my kids get themselves tangled in some kind of fight or squabble that they don't have the language or emotional resources to figure out on their own, so I have to step in and help them work through it. In so doing, I hope I help equip them little-by-little with resources of their own. After all, our goal as parents is to help our kids become fully-functioning adults to the point where we are no longer such central figures in their lives.

***

It's always bothered me for reasons I couldn't explain at first when I saw women using pictures of their kids as their only profile picture on social media. Some men may do this also, but it's much rarer at least in my circle of a few thousand connections across a couple of platforms. It's as though in the midst of the goal to eventually fade out of our children's lives in terms of the centrality of their needs, mothers also fade out of their own lives and become reoriented almost entirely towards their children at the expense of their own goals, dreams, and desires. I realized at some point that it's an erasure. As though women exist to bring children into this world and then are supposed to slowly disappear out of existence except to act as grandparents to help raise their offspring's eventual offspring. No career, no interests, no individual life is needed. This is why women who break this norm however that looks are viewed as dangerous and transgressive. It's why God can't be mother, only father, at least in white, evangelical, American Christianity because we have no concept of what a woman even is after they become a mother.

I experienced discomfort with this moving from baby shower to birth and beyond. All too often after I had procreated, people forgot I existed. While they talked to me, it wasn't like I wasn't there. They had no questions to ask me that didn't relate to my children or my husband, no observations to make outside of that except the occasional inappropriate comment on my weight loss after my second pregnancy. I had accomplished all that our society asks of women. I'd gotten married, produced two children, and was appropriately shrinking my body down to not take up as much space. Go me.

I noticed again recently how so many stories are coming of age stories, kids without parents stories, as though parents are simply a vessel to bring their children into the world, but who must be done away with in order for the kids to have an adventure. Of course some of this is just logistical. As a parent writing a pre-teen adventure story myself a few years ago, I realized the parents couldn't come along because good parents don't let their kids go off into the woods alone for extended periods of time to try to save the world. So I imprisoned them via the big bad and left it at that. But the overall theme is still there. Adventures are for the young, parents are supposed to only exist for their children, you're supposed to "settle down"—whatever that means.

One of my favorite series of books as a preteen was the Anne of Green Gables series. I'd loved growing up with Anne, but I remember on one of my re-reads a vague sense of foreboding. You see, the series follows Anne through adulthood, marriage, and then children, but after she has children, the series changes and starts narrating things through her children's perspectives almost exclusively. The interior life of Anne over forty is something we only get one tiny glimpse of throughout the final books. She becomes not Anne but "Mother," and we follow her children's adventures after that. There are evidently no adventures after children, there's only caring for them and shrinking into the background of their stories.

Perhaps this is why as I've crossed the threshold of forty myself, I've felt a deeply buried panic attempting to struggle to the surface at times. I've resisted looking at it until an attempt to live my own story created a space for it to surface with a vengeance and forced me to look at it full in the face.

***

My glasses were fogging near non-stop as the rain poured down on me. Everything was dripping, my clothes, my pack, my hair, the trees. I slid the pack off my shoulders onto a bench by the fire pit, but had no time to appreciate feeling that much lighter because the sun was setting, and I only had a few minutes to assess my location and decide where to set up my hammock. Too many of the trees towards the back of the site had dead limbs I decided after several impatient swipes at my glasses. For some reason my sunglasses don't fog and had been my choice for hiking that day, but the late hour and the storm rendered them more dangerous than my foggy situation with my regular glasses. "You are strong, smart, and prepared. You make good decisions," I reminded myself mentally. I selected two trees that were just barely far enough apart to work, closer to the lake, and away from all the ones with dead limbs.

The work focused me. The light was failing and while I had a fully-charged headlamp in my possession, it is still easier to set up with enough light to see. I quickly got my rain tarp stretched and pegged out and added a footprint tarp beneath, which created a narrow channel of dryness amidst the otherwise unrelenting wet. I quickly pulled my pack underneath the shelter so I could set up my hammock, bug net, underquilt, and pull out the backpacking stove and titanium mug that served as my kitchen to prepare my supper.

As I sat down on my tarp and lit my stove, I was hit with an overwhelming wave of homesickness. Just why did I feel the need to hike into the middle of the woods by myself anyway? I was convinced I needed some alone time, a quiet respite in the midst of raising two adorable and constantly noisy children. I was testing my gear and my resolve. After all, I planned to take the kids backpacking at some point too, and I wanted to work out any kinks on my own before I needed to look after them as well.

Hiking out was no option no matter how I felt. The almost six-mile trek back to my car had already been turned into a river as I sloshed the last two miles to the campsite, and it was still raining heavily. The last light from the sun faded from the sky with no glorious colors or ceremony: it just fizzled as though extinguished by the downpour.

I boiled my water and added it to a freeze-dried backpacking meal that had sounded good in the store. A few minutes later I learned that one should never take an untested brand or meal with you as this meal managed to somehow be simultaneously too spicy and flavorless. I pressed the air out of it after choking down maybe a quarter of its contents, zipped it shut, stuffed it in the gallon ziplock that was my trash bag, and glared at the now rehydrated and therefore much heavier meal I would have to pack back out.

The breeze off the lake was hitting me and despite the overnight lows not dipping below seventy degrees Fahrenheit, I started to feel chilly. I stood up and stripped off my wet layers, drying off with my compact microfiber towel, and learned sometimes just being dry over being wet is a huge mood boost. I sat on my towel to keep my leggings dry and munched a backup breakfast bar as I watched the rain drip off the edge of the tarp.

I couldn't seem to process the waves of emotion hitting me. I couldn't understand them. I had been so excited for my first real backpacking trip, even if it was a practice run at a state park close to home. Me being me, I had researched meticulously, chosen gear at the best nexus of being affordable and lightweight enough that the combined load would be doable. I had planned this trip weeks in advance, had planned to go alone if need be, even though an acquaintance first said she'd come along, only to bail the morning of the actual trip. I'd planned for the rain, my plans were sound, and I was now dry and warm and fed.

I'd expected to feel empowered and badass, but that night all I felt was a rising question of why I was sitting here in the rain instead of cozy at home with my family. What was it? I don't subscribe to the notion that mothers can't go off and do things for themselves or on their own, at least not consciously. I was refusing to disappear behind my children, refusing to become the older Anne in the books that has no interior life or goals beyond the raising of children. I just didn't know it would feel so transgressive this first trip out.

I am sure there is more to life after motherhood than disappearing behind endless rounds of dishes and laundry and activities for my kids only. I didn't really care that several people I'd told about this trip were completely confused and/or worried about my plan to do this on my own despite the fact that this time I even had cell phone signal in addition to the emergency sos capability on my watch. A few weeks before I'd hiked a much more difficult trail in a much more remote location with no signal, but no one worried about that one because it was a day hike with a friend.

Was that it? Was this confused emotion because I was breaking with societal conventions and doing the thing that women aren't supposed to do—especially if they have children. Here I was alone—at night—in the woods. And yet I didn't feel unsafe at all. The idea that this was dangerous only seemed plausible from well-lit living rooms where people don't intentionally venture out when there's a better than fifty percent chance of rain.

The rain mostly stopped, and I climbed into my hammock. I love sleeping in my hammock even though at this point, I'd only had the chance to do it a few times. It is indescribably cozy in a hammock. It feels like a nest, with the underquilt keeping the breeze from chilling me as I lay there. The silky outer fabric of my down top quilt is a sensory feast to my skin. The rain started again, and I remembered how much I love listening to the rain on a tarp or tent, the night air cooling around me, the scents of the forest brought to life by the water.

Lying there the doubt and negative emotions faded and I was truly glad to be there, looking forward to waking up by the lake in the early morning, seeing what the next day would bring. Getting up to pee in the middle of the night revealed that the lake looked like an enormous silver mirror. Despite the fact that it was light pollution from nearby Nashville lighting up the clouds to reflect on the lake and produce that effect, it looked magical. "Now there," I thought to myself, "that's something you couldn't see by day-hiking."

I woke at 6:30, surprised I'd actually slept so well I'd made it an hour past sunrise. I'd planned to have a leisurely morning, sipping my two cups of camp pour-over coffee on a rock by the lake and processing all the things I'd been feeling, but a text from a friend got me to check the weather. I realized if I didn't want to be caught in an unscheduled thunderstorm, I needed to break camp and hoof it back to the car. Slogging through the rain with all my gear two days in a row might be a necessary skill for future long hikes, but on a two-day trip, I didn't care to repeat it. So I drank one cup of coffee and ate half of my rehydrated scrambled eggs and bacon as I folded, wrapped, and stuffed my gear back into a compact state. I quickly assessed my water and decided I had enough for the return trip without the time-intensive process of filtering and treating the lake water to make it safe for me to drink.

About half-way back to the car, an airy slurp on the tube of my water reservoir told me I had miscalculated in my rush, or perhaps as I hadn't stopped at all to rest, I was using water faster than I had the day before. I was now nowhere near where I could access the lake easily, so I pressed on. By the time I'd wound back around and down to the lakeshore, I realized that I was less than two miles from my car. If I treated the water from the lake, it would take thirty minutes to be able to drink it, and I was maybe forty-five minutes from the car. Plus I remembered I had about a third a liter of smart water left, but I decided to save that until I was closer. I crossed a dry stream bed less than a mile and a half from the car and stopped and drank exactly half of my remaining water. Then I pushed on, covering the next mile a tad slower than usual, but not by much. I should interject I was now on the part where the backcountry trail intersects with a wider, much more highly trafficked day-loop trail that at this point I'd walked several times. The chances of getting lost with no water were almost zero, and with distant thunder rumbling, I pushed on. In a different situation, I would have stopped to filter regardless to make sure I didn't run out of water.

When I reached the sign where the trail split and I knew I was only half a mile from the trailhead, I sat on a bench and downed the last of the smart water. Buoyed by the electrolytes, I made the final push to the car. I'd never been so happy to see my sixteen-year-old, slightly oxidized Camry in my life. I shoved my gear into the passenger side and sank with relief into my seat. Then I made a beeline for McDonalds where I drank the best tasting bottle of water and ate the most delicious bacon, egg, and cheese biscuit I've ever had. Oh, and the thunderstorm opened the heavens about 10 minutes after I reached my car, which told me that in the circumstances, I had made the right call.

The day after the trip I felt amazing. Refueled with some good protein and loads of electrolytes, I was barely even sore. I also started feeling exhilarated and like the bad-ass I thought I'd experience myself as on the trail. I was still Mom, but now I was beginning to feel more like Anna again too.

INWARD APOCALYPSE: UNCOVERING A FAITH FOR THE COMMON GOOD

***

Accepting God as mother instead of only father can pave the way to eradicating false dichotomies created by society's gendered expectations. After all Jesus saves us in his humanity, not in his maleness. This should be obvious, but Jesus' biological sex seems to be a hangup among the groups that argue only men can stand before the congregation and say "this is my body." The arguments against women in leadership stem mostly from patriarchal societal expectation layered with a thin veneer of supposed theology where Jesus' biological sex is forever a roadblock to women with callings.

Seeing that God transcends gender and the biological sex of Jesus is incidental to theology shows us salvation isn't gendered, it's human. Because that's what it really comes down to in the crux of it. Saying women can't simply because they're women implies women are not fully redeemed nor redeemable. And that's not even broaching the topic of non-binary folks also being fully the image of God and fully redeemable.

In the final examination, it matters that I am a woman because it's part of who I am. But that fact doesn't dictate anything beyond the biological level. My abilities and interests aren't gendered nor are my limitations or lack thereof.

It is no more transgressive for me to want to hike or backpack alone than it is for my husband. And as I live into a life unbounded by society's expectations of what I should or shouldn't do, I pray the expansiveness of God's salvation becomes ever more visible as I learn to look for it. Like blazes on a trail, what we see in Scripture points us in the direction of a love that is big enough to save us all, include us all, and equip us all to be more fully human the way we were meant to be. As I've reached this stage of my journey, I am realizing that all the unpacking I have been doing to shed the layers of toxic theology that my early understandings of the gospel was wrapped in has not only helped me embrace the belovedness and full humanity of other people: it is helping me embrace my own belovedness and the fullness of my own humanity.

Section Two: Embodiment

Inward Apocalypse: Uncovering a Faith for the Common Good

you shouldn't
have to walk
the road to emmaus
to finally believe
a woman's
story

and what i
would give
for jesus
to call you out
on your violent
misogyny
instead of just
engaging
your faulty
theology

because women
shouldn't be
amazing you
they should be
leading you
too

and what i
would give
for jesus
to refuse to
eat dinner
until you apologized
instead of moving
so quickly
to open
your eyes because men
who break bread

without breaking
supremacy
shouldn't get
to socialize
with saviors
without
any
accountability

and we're no
strangers
to silence
or doubt
when men
write the story
women are always
left out

but sure
keep walking
and talking
about those
women
amazing you
god doesn't care
he's too busy
placating
you
–Kaitlin Shetler

6

Emmaus

The day Juneteenth was first observed as a federal holiday, I was wandering Chattanooga, TN by myself waiting for a friend. I hadn't been to this city in fourteen years and I was in a district filled with hip restaurants, bakeries, and mostly white people. I was early, so I took a walk. They called this the "historic district" when I was looking for a restaurant online, but nothing looked particularly historic to me.

In November of 2019, I participated in Freedom Road's Ruby Woo pilgrimage, and now I was putting into practice something I learned during that time. I was moving around an area to get a feel for what was going on and trying to see beyond the advertised shine to the undercurrents of the systems in the city. I'm not sure who decided the boundaries exactly of this so-called historic district, but here it was, spreading outwards from the freeway exit with its shiny glass fronts and retro-fitted industrial buildings. Around the perimeter of that there were new house builds, some of them right up against the old houses. The new houses stuck out because of their bright and trendy colors, rendering the older houses drab and shabby by comparison. Except for the bright green of the late spring trees and plants, there was almost an illusion of a color picture next to a black and white one. And like so many black-and-white images of the civil rights movement, the lack of color seems to trick our brain into assigning things in black and white in the past, as in "it's past, there's nothing we can do about it." Meanwhile, the truly "historic district" of this downtown neighborhood is being slowly consumed right in front of our eyes by gentrification: a posh cover word for pushing people of color out of downtown neighborhoods and "reclaiming" in the name of improvement and systematic white supremacy.

While historic practices of redlining are no longer as explicit as they once were, city management, developers, and even real estate agents continue to help enforce them in unspoken, but obvious ways when you know what to look for. "White flight" decades ago left urban areas in the hands of people of color and cities devalued properties in these areas and refused to invest in infrastructure, instead diverting those funds to the "better" read "white" neighborhoods.

Fresh from a two-and-a-half hour drive, I headed into a bakery. My stomach still full of sixteen ounces of Starbucks' Pike Place that I'd slowly consumed on the drive, I settled on a lavender thyme spritzer (herb-infused sparkling water), and headed outside to the patio covered with beams and a corrugated transparent plastic roof that had vines slowly growing on wires underneath for shade. There was a little fountain as the centerpiece for this courtyard, made of rust-colored scoops welded together, water trickled down them pleasantly, occasionally splashing me as I sat there.

I'd forgotten my notebook, so I opened the Google docs app on my phone and started thumb typing as fast as I could to catch the thoughts that were coming as I tried to start framing a chapter on supremacy and the implications of communion in the midst of this gentrified neighborhood. Conversations ebbed and flowed around me. As voices rose for emphasis or excitement, I'd sometimes catch bits and pieces particularly from this group of women behind me. Phrases about someone they couldn't believe was doing something mixed with church-y lingo about prayer and blessings. I couldn't catch whole conversations but the scraps of words floated by as I considered church and supremacy in this spot, wondering who had been displaced to make room for this tranquil courtyard. Was this like Central Park on a smaller scale? Central Park in Manhattan was built on the bulldozed ruins of a thriving Black community, a scene that has played out over and over in different ways around different cities, and one that continues to play out to this day in places like the so-called historic district I was now sitting in.

And here I was, hanging in the bakery, starting work on this chapter, meeting a friend at the restaurant next door and benefiting from the displacement of the residents of this neighborhood. I was breaking bread with my friends, but in doing so, was I contributing to supremacist culture?

***

"Because men who break bread without breaking supremacy shouldn't get to socialize with saviors without any accountability." This line from Kaitlin Shetler's poem "Emmaus" has been stuck in my head since the first time I read it. It's really easy for me to picture these two men walking down the road to Emmaus discussing the latest conspiracy theories about Jesus' crucifixion and supposed resurrection. If only they'd been able to hear from a credible witness or if one of their group had seen the resurrection first hand or something, then maybe they could be certain. Oh wait. That's exactly what had happened. Only the eye-witnesses to the resurrection were women.

In the culture of the time, women could not serve as legal witnesses in court, so there's a part of me that understands the doubt of these men and yet I still find myself angry and disappointed. These weren't just random people, they knew the women that were claiming to be witness to the resurrection. But they couldn't figure out if they should be believed because of the extreme devaluing of women in the society.

This is the day of the resurrection. The women have returned from the tomb proclaiming that Jesus had risen, just as he said he would, and the men of the group dismiss their story as "an idle tale."[1] These two men are leaving Jerusalem, indicating that perhaps the company of the disciples is already breaking up in the wake of the crucifixion because they wouldn't listen to what Jesus had told them was his true purpose, and they wouldn't believe the female disciples in their group. In their hubris, one of them, the text calls him Cleopas, actually attempts to explain the commotion around the events of the crucifixion and resurrection to Jesus. Jesus walked up next to them—in person—on the road out of Jerusalem, and they failed to recognize him.

I've always taken great comfort in the fact that Jesus chose to reveal himself to the women first. He was unencumbered by the status

---
[1] Luke 24:11 NRSV

quo of women in that day and treated them as the full humans he knew they were with no reference to contingencies in order to convince the rest of the folks at the time.

There's lessons here for us. While progress is incremental, we as the church are called to live like Jesus. Instead of asking people to wait their turn, we should be pushing society to treat all people with equity and justice, and we should be modeling that ourselves as those who claim to follow Christ. Unfortunately, the church in America has much to answer for as American Christianity especially in the form of the white evangelical church that so many of us have had to abandon, has all too often done the exact opposite in terms of harboring and fostering white supremacy and all forms of homophobia and sexism. And not just harboring, but all too often these supremacies are backed up with false theological support that manipulates some into believing it, and/or provides handy justification to those who want to believe that anyway.

***

"What's the makeup of the group?" He asked me. I was taken aback. He was referring to this group of mostly ten and eleven-year olds that we ran more like a youth group than a Sunday school class, and the makeup he was asking about was the racial makeup.

"I couldn't tell you for sure," I responded probably a tad pompously if I'm honest with my recollection. After all, why did it matter what the racial makeup was, right? These were all just kids and I cared for them equally. I didn't see them as Black, or European, or Latino, or Asian. And yes, we had kids of all those descriptors in one church as this was a white-run congregation in a neighborhood that had experienced white flight and yet the church had stayed and the white people just kept driving back. That was before my time, so I don't know all the dynamics of that, just that the people who lived around the church, some of whom sent their kids but didn't attend themselves, were mostly immigrant communities from Central America.

And yet I don't ever recall discussing racism or the social dynamics at play in this church. I certainly was never prompted to confront answers such as the one I described above which dangerously close to the "I don't see color" trope. I felt smug and non-racist by refusing to quantify the races of the kids I worked with, but in doing so, what was I missing about their lives and situations outside of our church-y little melting pot where all were supposed to be equal.

The only time I remember race being mentioned was when this church—so large that it already had two locations on the same street "east" and "west" campuses—decided to open a "north" campus in a different valley from its historical location. The senior pastor at the time said adamantly that this wasn't a "white flight" campus. However, the new location was in the white valley, the one people had started moving to several decades earlier as this valley became more and more diverse. I remember feeling that it was a bad move even though I didn't understand the dynamics of white flight and gentrification because I'd never been in an environment to talk about these terms.

***

The balcony that ran around the courtyard of the second floor sloped away from the wall with the rows of doors. I wondered for multiple reasons if I was quite safe though there were plenty of people walking on this sloping ground as if they were used to it and didn't expect it to fall at any moment. I had driven one of the kids from this late elementary ministry home that day, and she'd invited me to come meet her mom who didn't come to church. I accepted, but knew that if my parents saw where I was, by myself, they'd be duly freaked out. I was in the bad part of town, in this derelict apartment building, gingerly stepping across this leaning balcony of certain death in my church shoes. But I was trying not to be rude, and I wanted to be sure this student made it safely to her door, so I continued. Almost all of the danger was imagined (the balcony was probably the only thing with any inherent danger). I have no idea how I came across to her mom as we tried to converse briefly across two languages with the help of an eager ten-year-old interpreter who was probably trying to blend her worlds together. Each of us was fluent in one, and barely spoke the other. I do know that was the only time I set foot there. I imagine my discomfort was probably obvious even though I tried to hide it. I can't remember if I sat down and if I did, did I barely perch on the edge of the couch the way you do when you think it's dirty, or don't want to stay too long? It's been so long that those details are fuzzier than the permanent impression that leaning balcony made on my memory.

I didn't have the tools then to parse my reaction or to start unpacking the layers of supremacies that undergirded it. After all, I was sharing Jesus with these kids, surely that was the most important? But what Jesus was I sharing? A Jesus that didn't care about predatory landlords who wouldn't fix balconies of certain death? A Jesus that sanctioned the white people not having to drive to the "dangerous" part of town so they didn't have to see the inequalities in our system or parse why there might be known gang activity not blocks from where they praised the Lord?

***

My family is supposedly related to the Dandridge family, meaning that by marriage, I'm related to both George Washington and Robert E. Lee. While the genealogy research done so far backs this up, whether it's true or not is less important than the way the lore played out in my family history. The way the story ran was the civil war was bad of course, and the idea of fighting for slavery was wrong, but Robert E. Lee was a gentleman and was fighting for Virginia not the South and therefore his mistake was somehow excusable. He was, in the lore, a much nicer person than that nasty General Grant.

All of this helped instill the idea that being a nice white person somehow canceled out the "mistake" of aligning with white supremacy and the actual enslavement of human beings. I mean, Lee didn't just join up and fight with other Virginians, he commanded the whole Confederate army. It's not like this was an oversight caused by peer pressure: he actively tried to make the South and slavery win the day. But he was a gentleman, so it's all okay?

This "nice white person" narrative I suspect was behind many people's motivations for attending that church in the middle of the city, the one now surrounded by what had become low-income housing and immigrant communities. But look where we were going to church. We couldn't possibly be racist.

I haven't gone back to visit since the opening of that north campus, you know, the one that wasn't the "white flight" campus. But I suspect the make-up of the attendees at the original locations has changed considerably. And that's much the loss of the folks that chose to leave. Being in relationship with people who are different from us is the start of understanding stories other than our own and establishing solidarity with those who are actively harmed by systems of injustice that perhaps we can't even see because they don't harm us.

I added this church and its environment to my resume in later years, proud of my accomplishments of working in such a place, as though my involvement was some kind of heroic endeavor, overlooking the real heroes: the ones who had created lives for themselves and their families despite the hostile conditions.

The founding pastor of this church, before he retired, once preached a sermon where the topic of masturbation came up. I distinctly remember the example he used. He said that people would ask him if masturbation was okay or not. Then he referenced people that argued that it's natural, it's a release, similar to blowing a stuffy nose. Then the clincher: he said that obviously that argument was false because he never had anyone come up and ask him if it was okay to blow one's nose. And then he shuffled on to a different topic, completely ignoring all of the strange mixed messages that church and culture have told people about their sexuality and their bodies as though we could just inherently know what was okay and what wasn't similar to deciding when our noses need to be blown. Or that we even would know when to blow our noses if we hadn't been taught at a young age when and how to do so. Arguing things from the inherent idea that you'll just know what's right and wrong is damaging because it assumes that we can somehow exist unaffected from all the messages from culture and the church that are designed to make us ashamed of our bodies and its functions.

Arguing that we can just somehow "know" things outside of community and conversation is also ultimately antithetical to how our lives are meant to be lived out. Which brings me back to the road to Emmaus and why Jesus would break bread with a couple of misogynists.

The male supremacy of the culture in Jesus' time was absolute. In Roman culture, the father of the household had the power of life or death over the members of his household, reducing his wife and dependent children to barely above the level of the enslaved members of the household, at least in terms of their dependence on keeping the man happy.

It is against this backdrop that Jesus calls women to be disciples, and then elevates these women, especially Mary Magdalene, to be the first apostles: ones who were sent to tell the good news of Jesus' resurrection to the male disciples who were largely cowering in fear behind locked doors afraid of the potential repercussions of following this Jesus who had been crucified.

And when the Cleopas and his friend admit that they didn't believe the women who told them that Jesus had risen, his immediate response is, "Oh, how foolish you are, and how slow of heart to believe all that the prophets have declared."[2] Joel B. Green in his commentary on Luke observes that here "foolish" means "obtuse." He goes on to point out that "This is not to say, however, that they are simply lacking cognitive input. 'Slow of heart' calls attention to their failure to orient themselves fully around Jesus' teaching... Failure of insight comes from failure to embrace the ways of God."[3]

There's a variety of things the prophets can refer to. The most obvious is the part of Scripture at the time that was collectively referred to as "the prophets." But prophetic texts—even though they are often interpreted as future-telling—had meaning for their own time as well: highlighting things that needed changing, calling out collective sins, and speaking truth to power.

The fact that this is Jesus' response to the men telling him they didn't believe the women (nor the men who had gone to check on the women's account), feels like Jesus is elevating the women to the status of prophet right in front of their eyes. This is consistent with the understanding that Mary Magdalene is the "apostle to the apostles" and that it indicates what Jesus believes about the status of women. Indeed, if the problem with these men is that their hearts weren't oriented towards the things of God and therefore they couldn't see

---

[2] Luke 24:25 NRSV
[3] Joel B. Green, *The Gospel of Luke*, 848.

what was plain in front of them, it stands to reason that one of the major problems with their hearts is they couldn't see that Jesus was treating women like equals and therefore they should as well.

I once was having a hard time with the church as a whole as the result of a decision to cut my position as diocesan-wide coordinator for youth and family ministries based on budgetary struggles following a contentious meeting. At the diocesan convention that year, I skipped the Eucharist. I followed my row up and then just by-passed the rail and went back to my seat. I was certain no one had spotted me, but an acquaintance of mine who was a priest did. He asked why I'd skipped the rail and I said I didn't feel like I was in fellowship with the people around me, and therefore shouldn't take communion. He told me I should never skip because communion was more a statement about what should be rather than what was. I don't think I'm quite doing justice to his actual words with my remembered paraphrase, but that was the gist of it. I didn't agree with him at the time, but his words stuck in my head. In more recent years, I've come to think that he was right.

Communion is about what should be rather than what is. But that's not just some aspirational pie-in-the-sky hopeful speak either. The act of taking communion is a commitment to work towards what should be rather than what is, even if we don't fully understand all that should be. The act of taking communion has implications for how we live our lives. It makes a statement about our values and the direction of our personal and our communal lives. It should not and cannot be taken lightly.

The breaking of the bread is about the broken body of Jesus who allowed himself to be broken by the systems of this world both to be in solidarity with those also broken by the unjust systems and to break those systems once and for all. The breaking of the bread is about the breaking of supremacies and our commitment to "embrace the ways of God."

*Adventure is not
given or earned.
She is a breath that is prayed,
a force that is found,
found in the soul of everyone
and everything.*
−Kaitlin Curtice, *A Rhythm of Prayer*, p. 107

7

Pilgrim

I stepped into the cool, hushed interior of the downtown church feeling slightly out of place. Ironically, this was my home church. I'd transferred my membership there over two years before, but the intervening pandemic had meant that I'd only gotten to attend in person for a year before everything shut down. But that wasn't why I felt out of place. I'd just never gone to church so dirty before. My hair was styled—if you can call it that—with sweat, hastily blow-dried by the air conditioner in my car as I drove over. I was trying to act natural while holding my arms away from my body so that the clean button-up shirt I'd put on over my still sweat-soaked tank top wouldn't show damp spots.

I walked into the tiny side chapel where the midday Eucharist was held to discover it was going to be just me and the priest and the iPad on a tripod streaming the service to people at home. I stepped carefully around the tripod and picked a seat I hoped was out of the frame. I was conscious of not leaning back on the seat because of the afore-mentioned sweaty tank-top.

Since March in the second spring of the pandemic, I had been virtually walking the Camino de Santiago, the longer Camino Frances or French way, beginning in St. Jean Pied de Port in France to Santiago de Compostela in Spain. The virtual pilgrimage was started by a group of Camino alumni who wanted to do something to support the albergues—hostels for pilgrims—that had been shuttered by the pandemic. So they created an app where participants could pay to participate in a virtual version from their own corners of the world and the money would go to support the struggling albergues.

The week I went to church dirty and sweaty was the final week of my virtual camino. When I looked at the app and realized I would finish on Friday no matter what I did, I decided I needed to do something more momentous to finalize the experience. So I started hiking at dawn that day, went nine miles through a small dedicated wilderness area north of Nashville, and then headed back to my car with the intention of going to church in my hiking clothes. I did a quick hiker sponge bath with one of my tiny compressed wipes. You pour water on them and they expand quickly into a full wipe after looking exactly like a large pill in a small tube. I'd brought my hair brush and deodorant to freshly apply after wiping all the smelliest bits of me down. So I'm mostly confident that I didn't smell at least; but they say you can't always smell yourself; and I confess that my car smelled after leaving my sweaty pack inside in the hot sun, so I can't really be sure I didn't also go to church smelly.

But hiking that morning and then going to church was the closest I could get to the pilgrim experience of walking into the cathedral in Santiago de Compostela after finishing my pilgrimage. I do think it's probably easier to go to church with a bunch of other sweaty people in a city where people have been going to church dirty for thousands of years, but on the other hand, it shouldn't really matter how we come to church.

It turned out marvelously for all my jitters. The priest didn't look askance at me at all, and was thrilled with what I'd been doing when I told her afterwards about the virtual camino. But she was welcoming to me before she knew who I was, and that's the more important bit.

Tackling something like a long-distance hike or pilgrimage, even virtually, provides numerous takeaways. When I first opened the map and looked at that impossibly long line stretching across the entire width of Spain, it seemed like I would never get to the end. But a pilgrimage is made up of miles and miles are made up of steps. And I learned that there's no such thing as too small an action to make a difference as long as we commit to consistency.

One of the most powerful things that a physical pilgrimage teaches you no matter how you undertake it is that little things add up. You could argue that a single step doesn't make a difference. But when you commit to one step and then one step and then one more, you see that steps turn into miles. Eventually, even if you've largely walked laps in your driveway, those steps turn into 485 miles and the length of the Camino Frances across the whole of Spain. I stared at the map on the app and my little icon there, on the threshold of Santiago, having colored in the line all the way across the country, a feat that seemed huge the beginning of March when I started, and here I was in the third week of June crossing the finish line.

I've also learned that hiking turns a number of popular aphorisms on their heads. When hiking, what goes down, has to hike back up. That morning I started out hiking up at the top of a bluff, having gotten there fairly easily because the trailhead I parked at was already more than halfway up. So when the trail began a lovely descent that quickly had me down in between the bluffs, I knew I was in for some hard work to get back up again. I paused at the bottom, next to a stream and realized that there's this lionization of mountain-top experiences as metaphors for faith as though the mountain is always good and uplifting, and the valley is always either bad or hard or at the very least, mundane. And while the views are better from the mountaintops, up there you are exposed to storms and elements and you can't stay. In the valleys there is shelter and water and flat places to camp.

Hiking back up to the next bluff, the breeze hit me and felt marvelous on this early summer day, and I realized that the idea of being sheltered from the wind is also one that is entirely relative depending on your perspective. If it was a cold day, coming up into that wind would have been chilling, and I would have welcomed the next descent into the next valley as a way to get a break from the cold. But on a day that was already over eighty by 9 am, the breeze cooled me off and provided a break from the relentless heat and higher humidity in the valleys.

In the same way, things we have long considered to be good or at least neutral in the systems of our world, can be harmful and toxic to others. This is essential to keep in mind when listening to stories of others. Whether some things are helpful or harmful can be entirely relative based on one's perspective, and only in listening to the stories of others can we really gain an understanding beyond our limited perspective.

If I had to boil pilgrimage down to its essential nature, I would say it's committing to something consistently that helps you get outside your own worldview. What that is and how it looks doesn't matter so much as long as that goal is being achieved. This is why I think it is possible to live life as a pilgrim, and find that kind of mindset whether or not one actually goes on any kind of official pilgrimage or not.

Of course official pilgrimages can be helpful because by definition they take you outside your normal life, sometimes far outside, and often push your physical limitations in some way as well. It didn't occur to me to try to live life as a pilgrim until after my experience on the Ruby Woo Pilgrimage, which while only four days long proved to be an immersive and life-changing experience.

One of the biggest things I learned from that experience actually began before I left. Some combination of internalized societal gender roles and expectations especially for mothers that I broke down in chapter five and my own struggles with anxiety left me in states of near panic multiple times before I left. These would often culminate before our pre-pilgrimage zoom meetings, and I would spend an hour or more pacing in my driveway, thinking and praying until it was time to log in. The meetings would inevitably imbue me with a sense of calm that would last a few days, only to have that feeling fall apart again in the face of rising anxiety as the next meeting approached.

But underneath the rising and falling tides of anxiety, I felt like the pilgrimage was something that was very important for me to do. My gut, that I was finally learning to trust, told me that this pilgrimage would be a catalyst on multiple levels. I wanted to do a deep dive into what it meant to be a pilgrim, and into the complicated history in our nation. I also wanted to be able to travel by myself again, something I had enjoyed in years previous, so I gritted my teeth, paced as much as I felt necessary, and managed to get on the plane. Once en route, I was fine.

I have experienced smaller versions of this as I prepared to hike solo and backpack solo, and occasionally even when I launched into new experiences with my family, such as taking my kids backpacking for the first time. But so far, one hundred percent of the time, it has been worth pushing through the anxiety and discomfort to the other side and experiencing something new.

This lesson goes beyond physical experiences to educational and worldview shifts as well. For example, leaning into the initial discomfort of discovering there were two creation stories in Genesis lead to freedom. Freedom often lies on the other side of discomfort. It's only when we make a habit of pushing through the discomfort, learning to live with the discomfort, and eventually embracing the discomfort that we begin to truly thrive and then seek the thriving of others. That state is what is referred to as shalom. And the road to get there is a pilgrim's road.

But this journey looks very different from the first pilgrimage I encountered as a child.

***

"Little Christian lived in a great city called Destruction. Its streets were full of boys and girls who laughed and played all day long."[1] So begins the retelling of Pilgrim's Progress for children, written by Helen L. Taylor. It proceeds to detail "grave-looking" strangers who would come and try to tell the children stories about a beautiful kingdom far away with a kind King who loves children. The warning that the strangers brought was about how their king was going to come and kill everyone in the city of destruction, and the only way to escape was for these children to leave everything they knew and go to the "celestial city" on their own.

This was my favorite book as a child. Re-reading it as an adult, I was horrified by this casual introduction of adults meeting the perfect child-predator profile. Then, on a different layer, understanding that this "king" was supposed to be Jesus, but the invite is "run away or you'll be murdered." I can't see the gospel anywhere in here.

The opening vilifies play in the first few lines and helped set me up for a life without rest, something it took me into my adult years to figure out was really quite an unhealthy mindset. Then by chapter three when little Christian finally decides to run away and try to go to the celestial city, two of his playmates run after him and try to convince

---

[1] Helen Taylor, *Little Pilgrim's Progress*, 9.

him to turn back. In a real world scenario, a child running away from his family and everyone he knows should be turned back. But the idea of finding truth that everyone else scoffs at is also embedded early in the story and sets up a child's mind to be programmed by fundamentalist thinking, something else that took me years to unpack long into adulthood. This pilgrimage of little Christian's is fraught with issues just in the first few pages, not the least of which is extreme binary thinking. There's no fixing the systems of oppression in the city of destruction because as I recalled my friend saying in the beginning of chapter four, "It's all gonna burn."

***

I sat down to reflect and rest a moment at the top of one of the bluffs where an old service road bisected the trail and made for some of the only level ground around. I looked down at my watch and realized I was exactly at 5.22 miles, or 0.02 past the mileage I needed to actually finish the camino. I was still several miles from the trailhead, and had seen exactly three humans at this point. Being in the middle of a long loop trail meant there was no one remotely nearby. No crowded square, no fellow pilgrims, no stone cathedral. Just the green canopy sparkling in the sunlight and an overly curious hornet that kept landing nearby and eyeing me. I was alone, but not lonely as it turned out. Since I'd mostly been walking and hiking with my family, it had taken me over three miles this day to get out of my own head and enjoy being exactly where I was and free to think thoughts and hear myself think as they say.

Obviously I hadn't actually walked the Camino de Santiago and there's no way to duplicate the experience. However the connections and experience afforded by walking the virtual version still offered up some rich thoughts and experiences and highlighted the idea of what makes a "real" pilgrimage.

Most of my walks have been in rural settings or actual hikes as I participated in this virtual pilgrimage. I read some stories and watched the movie with Martin Sheen called The Way, about a father who walks the Camino after his son dies in a freak accident attempting the very same journey. One of the common threads I saw in Camino stories and even in the Facebook group was the question of what makes a "real" pilgrim. I see this kind of question in Appalachian trail groups and stories too. What makes a "real" thru-hiker? And while many will agree upon an arbitrary definition like finishing the whole trail in one 12-month unit of time, I wonder about this apparent need to attach validation to things like pilgrimages or thru-hikes. Surely these things have value in just doing them whether you finish them in one go or take it in sections. And it's not necessarily about the length of the trail either.

I've read good and transformative memoirs about hiking the Wonderland Trail, about 90 miles, the John Muir Trail in California, about 211 miles, and even stories of people who walked sections of the Appalachian trail instead of all 2190 miles (as it stands as of this writing, the length changes over the years due to necessary re-routes and so forth). And then there's the people experiencing transformation on this virtual camino experience just walking in their area for a few miles a day. Or thinking transformative thoughts walking loops in their driveways as I am known to do when I can't get out for an actual walk or hike somewhere.

Walking in my driveway and seeing how steps still add up to miles was one of the most humbling things about attempting the virtual camino. Without the camino to log miles in, I might have been less motivated to still walk up and down the steep incline of my driveway, determined to hit at least my average every day, even in the rain or the heat and humidity. I'd joke that it was like a real camino that way, throw on my rain jacket and keep going.

And while it would be silly to claim I've walked the Camino de Santiago without ever setting foot in Spain, I don't think it's silly at all to claim "real" pilgrim status. I think pilgrimage is a mindset. You could probably walk the real Camino and not be a pilgrim, though I don't think the definition has to do with how many miles you walk or how much help you get, or how authentic your journey is.

***

I was standing at the desk at the airport mortified because I'd missed my flight. Reluctant to leave my boyfriend, we'd dawdled too long in his truck before coming in and they would no longer allow me to board. I could choose to camp in the airport for an unknown period of time or pay a change fee and simply get on the same flight the next day. I chose the second option, and rode away from the airport in silence. I felt terrible that we'd driven all the way there for nothing, and I was also terrified that because I'd missed the plane I was supposed to be on, that something terrible would happen to me. The plane would crash or something because I'd been careless. This idea seems laughable to me now sixteen years or so later, but it is also sobering to think I still felt this well into my twenties.

I have to wonder how much I was influenced by my favorite childhood read in this sense. The people who didn't follow the instructions to get from the City of Destruction to the Celestial City had terrible things happen to them. Most of them ended up dead. When Christian strayed from the path, he was captured by a giant and had to escape. Taylor really made sure the idea of staying on the "straight and narrow" was personified in her story. And here I was, in my mid 20s, still convinced if I didn't do everything right, I'd fall victim to a terrible fate. I'm sure purity culture was also rearing its ugly head as we'd been kissing in the parking lot and therefore lost track of time. How dare I let myself be so distracted?

There was this sense growing up whether it was in Little Pilgrim's Progress or other places like the sermon I once heard that preached on the Bible verse about the acceptable, good, and perfect will of God as though those were attainable levels, that God would only protect you if you followed everything you were supposed to follow as perfectly as you possibly could. In some ways, this appealed to my personality. Give me a course syllabus and I would use it as a roadmap from here to an A. Lists I can check off are still something that gives me a sense of control knowing I've done all the things.

But life in this uncertain world is certainly not like that. You can't checklist your way out of the dangers of living on a broken and beautiful planet surrounded by broken and beautiful people. Nor are bad things happening to you a punishment for your unfaithfulness.

Taylor's text mirrored the teachings I was hearing in church and elsewhere in this bubble I was in growing up: it was my job to find my way into the straightest and narrowest interpretation of God's will and then stay there, or I would be in grave danger and terrible things would happen to me. Of course the implication of this is that when something bad happened, it would be my fault. Something bad happening to me meant I was in the wrong place either literally or spiritually or both.

In the book, the little pilgrims are physically punished, either by bad things happening, by a character named Justice who looks for pilgrims to beat if they've strayed only held back by the Prince, or by one of the Shining Ones administering corporal punishment with an actual whip. The author clearly had no sense of God's justice as being a good thing. For Taylor, justice is all inflexible punishment and stands in opposition to grace and mercy as opposed to all three being part of the same characteristic of God.

***

The week before I attempted my first Trailblaze challenge—a hiking marathon fundraiser for Make-A-Wish—I was wandering around a green space waiting for my oldest son to finish a class he was taking. I was in the rest week stage of training, where you don't want to do anything too strenuous. So instead of trying to push out some miles, I meandered taking pictures and exploring several side trails I hadn't even realized were there. I found tadpoles and ducks, a hidden pond complete with a beaver dam and a grumpy blue heron (though in its defense, I did make it miss a catch while I was trying to take its picture). I spent that week becoming a big fan of the side quest, something I hadn't been terribly good at while training because I was so focused on miles and pacing and hydration strategies.

Of course the very idea of a side quest means you're deviating from the most direct path to whatever the main goal is supposed to be. In Taylor's book, both side quests and rest are literal dangers to Christian getting to the celestial city. Her book has big "I can rest when I'm dead" energy.

But our lives don't have trail maps, and they aren't supposed to be a death march from birth to, well, death. We're supposed to meander and find wildflowers and take naps and stop for conversations. These things aren't distractions from our pilgrimages, rather, they are part of it. Our lives are not currency to be spent, nor commodities to be used. Pilgrimage as a mindset teaches us the journey is ever ongoing.

Without fail, transformative weekends such as the Ruby Woo pilgrimage have been beginnings—catalysts—for continued growth. Training for a hiking marathon taught me that recovery is literally part of training, that pushing yourself beyond your existing limits and then resting is how you build stronger muscles for the next challenge.

This is why a pilgrimage mindset is a vital part of our spiritual formation. It shows us the power of the small and consistent over the big and shiny. It shows us that we are on a journey of discovery, and sometimes side quests reveal a new main quest to pursue for a while. And it gives us a mandate to rest in cycle with our work, not as a distraction, but as a part of the work itself.

Reading the accounts of human walking, it is easy to begin to think of the Fall in terms of the falls, the innumerable spills, possible for a suddenly upright creature that must balance all its shifting weight on a single foot as it moves.
—Rebecca Solnit, *Wanderlust*, p. 33

8

Numbers

I stretched my legs as I climbed from the tiny hatchback. Five hours of driving from the southernmost tip of England to one of the northernmost sections had left me cramped and achy even at twenty-two. Two large tents capable of seating hundreds of people were set up in two nearby fields, their long, white canvas sides contrasting with the old stone of the buildings that had stood for hundreds of years. This was the Keswick Convention, and I was the only American hired as a youth counselor that year. A friend of the family was connected with the Convention and had recruited me to come over for two weeks and help out.

Twenty years later the details of these two weeks are still fairly crisp in my mind. Extended travel in other countries tends to slow time down and make every experience stand out crisply. The counselors were a group of mostly twenty-somethings, housed in two wings of a Victorian-style building that while renovated in Victorian times, dated back to the turn of the 18th century, or about as old as the country I came from. This was a short walk via roads and a path through a forest section from the headquarters of the Keswick convention in town and the fields just outside where the meeting tents were set up.

I dropped my backpacking pack and enormous wheeled duffel bag urged on me by parents who thought I wouldn't do laundry, I suppose, in a room with four sets of bunk beds set up. There were only to be four of us in the room; so as I recall, we all claimed bottom bunks. I'd met one of my roommates upon arrival; and after dropping off my things, I headed back down to find her standing silently with two young men in a semicircle. When she didn't move to introduce me, I stuck out my hand to the nearest guy and said, "Hey, I'm Anna."

I didn't understand the bemused smiles at first as I shook hands with both the guys. My roommate laughed and said, "Trust the American to just introduce herself."

Surprised, I replied, "Wait, so you didn't exchange names?"

And that's when I learned it was still common in England to wait to be introduced. I laughingly introduced the guys to my roommate, and the four of us hung out all week in our downtime, so it must not have been too big a cultural gaff.

That summer I spent nearly an entire month abroad, leaving after my two weeks in Keswick, bumming a ride off a fellow counselor to London where he dropped me at a train station so I could return to my friends' home in the south of England, only to fly out a few days later to Switzerland to meet up with my brother and a friend of ours who had been in France for a week while I finished my assignment at the Keswick convention. We then spent a week in Florence, Italy before meeting my parents in Rome for a final week. We did all this without international cell phones.

I returned to the Los Angeles area where I was living at the time and felt bombarded by bill boards. The city itself seemed to teem in ways that London or Florence or Rome never did. I remember thinking traveling was essential to making you see things you'd gotten so used to that you forgot how to see them.

I'm no longer certain it has to be physical travel, but rather a willingness to travel through the experiences of others: travel via the stories of people in our lives, travel via books even, so we can learn to see through the eyes of others.

***

When I began research for this chapter, I went looking for a specific quote from Amy Carmichael, an Irish missionary to India. I have found it beneficial to reread books from my childhood and youth to see with adult eyes the works that had an influence on me, and a children's biography of hers was something that I read over and over again before moving on to an adult biography. I couldn't find the exact one I'd had as a child, but I still dove back into her story and discovered that the Keswick Convention was her original sponsoring body.

Something like electricity ran through me. Participating in the Keswick Convention was a formative experience and while it didn't singularly affect the course of my life in the same way it did Amy's, discovering this tie to the same organization did something I can't completely verbalize.

You see, the quote I was looking for was this: "One can't save and then pitchfork souls into heaven."[1] This was in response to criticism from some of her donors that she was building houses and a hospital in rural India. After going there and living with other missionaries, she found herself unsettled at the way they insisted on maintaining their British lifestyles, ones which were completely divorced from the people they claimed to serve.

While there are inherent issues with the idea of missions by colonizing western nations, Amy moved past many of the expectations of her day, adopting Indian clothes and moving in with Indian Christians to do the work she felt called to do. She and her band of mostly female locals with a few other British nationals ended up adopting hundreds of children who would otherwise have been sold to the temples, many of whom would have ended up trafficked for the benefit of the temples.

She received criticism for doing this work instead of focusing on just "saving souls," but the quote above was her reply. As someone who lived with chronic illness, she knew all too well that the soul could not be divorced from the body, but rather, we humans are a complete package and both must be attended to. As someone who later developed a chronic illness (actually, three chronic illnesses, let it never be said that I am an underachiever!), this idea of soul and body together stuck with me as I learned to manage my conditions and slowly unlearned the internalized toxic capitalism that would make me think I was only as valuable as what I could produce, instead of having inherent value just by existing.

Ironically, white American Christianity both embraces the toxic capitalism and simultaneously believes that the work of the church is all "heart work" that somehow has no societal impact other than the

---
1 Elisabeth Elliot, *A Time to Die*, 247..

saving of souls. This is perhaps something of an over-simplification. However, if we boil things down to their essentials, it is fairly on target. Just in recent years the idea of challenging systemic racism and white supremacy has been met with pushback from white Christians who declare that racism is a "heart issue" and people just need Jesus to change their hearts. Sick? We don't need universal health coverage: we just need people to learn to trust Jesus for their healing. Interested in protecting children? And by that I mean ones outside the womb vulnerable to the Delta variant of Covid 19 as another wave of the pandemic swept the nation? Absolutely not, after all, wearing a mask or getting vaccinated is a sign of "living in fear" and apparently not trusting God.

To those raised outside of these circles, the amount of mental gymnastics needed to hold these positions seems untenable, but if we look at the decades upon decades of emphasis on the individual and that individual's heart, at least some of the pattern begins to emerge.

As Dominique Gilliard said, "Within too many congregations, repentance is defined and practiced as merely oral confession."[2] This follows along from an insistence that salvation is defined as "asking Jesus into your heart" both of which show a complete separation from the idea that true change of heart will be accompanied by a change in behavior. Now there are certain ideas about behavior that are supposed to change, but from my upbringing they are all categorized as personal issues for the most part such as not drinking or smoking or going to R-rated movies or not using swear-words.

I find it incredibly ironic that the children's show Daniel Tiger has a better grasp on repentance than most white evangelical churches. They even set it to music: "Saying I'm sorry is the first step, now how can I help?" In this simple tune, the idea that verbally acknowledging the wrong is only one part, and it must be accompanied by actions to help make things right.

After all, faith without works is dead, right? But how did this notion of good works showing one's faith get so twisted? It's as though in white evangelical circles, all the "good works" is about passing some purity test of "right" beliefs. What's more is that both right belief, right action, and sin have all become about what I the individual believe

---

2 Dominique Gilliard, *Subversive Witness: Scripture's Call to Leverage Privilege*, xviii.

and do as if what I the individual believe and do has no bearing on my community and society as a whole. Except of course, for pet issues like abortion where they insist they know better, or same-sex marriage which they insist is ungodly according to them therefore no one should be able to do it, and so on.

It's a double standard of mind-blowing proportions when you step back and think about it. To insist that they alone have a monopoly on what is individual and what is communal would be laughable hubris if they hadn't managed to work themselves into power and rig the system to stay there. This isn't the space to talk about strategies of race-based voter suppression, but there's plenty of resources to learn about that. What I'm concerned with here is how our faith, for those who call ourselves Christians, affects how we interact with our community and the larger society.

It doesn't seem like a stretch to say that we should work for the thriving of all people. We should work for a world where medical bankruptcy doesn't leave people unhoused, where addiction is treated like an illness and not a crime, where diabetics don't die because they were rationing insulin, where parents don't watch their asthmatic child die in their arms on the way to the emergency room because they couldn't afford the inhaler that month. These should be things that people who claim to follow the crucified and risen Christ should care about and fight to make better.

If you care about abortion, why not fight for a society where no woman ever feels like she has to have an abortion because of financial reasons?[3] Where there is proper healthcare, birth control, prenatal and postnatal care? Where there are safe, quality childcare options so the mom can finish school, and go to work, and care for her child? If that world existed, then abortions would only be necessary in extreme medical conditions, and women and their doctors could arrive at those decisions with dignity and privacy, and we wouldn't need legislation about it at all. And women and children could truly thrive. That's a country that cares about its children. Not one that as I write this is fighting mask mandates in schools even as our pediatric ICU beds fill to overflowing, where my friend's child who fell off the monkey bars

---

3 According to a study done by the Guttmacher Institute, 73% of women who get an abortion list finances as one of or the only reason.

at school and broke their arm had to wait six hours to be seen because the emergency rooms are overflowing with Covid and RSV cases.

They say that the United States is the land of the free, but it never has been. For one, most of the freedoms have only been really extended to white men. Historically, it was white male landowners, and in our current reality, just rich, white males. Everyone else has varying degrees of fewer rights depending on economic standing, race, sex, gender, etc. And two, we are never really free to do whatever anyway. We make laws about driving and traffic patterns. We have laws against stealing and murder and all sorts of other things that infringe upon our freedoms to do whatever we like. I might think I can safely drive ninety miles an hour anywhere, but I don't have that freedom because I not only risk myself, but the safety of others on the road if I behave like that.

Watching season five of the Expanse, Wes Chatham's character Amos Burton makes a comment that civilization tends to keep people civil. Without the first, you can't count on the second. And it does raise the question of what do we owe our neighbor? What does it say to our neighbor if we claim to care about the status of their eternal soul, but nothing about the state of their bodies and lives in the here and now?

Traveling abroad made me question things I took for granted. At one time I was looking at moving to England for graduate study, and was pleasantly surprised to discover my student status would grant me access to healthcare for as long as I had a student visa. No purchasing of additional insurance needed. There was and is a surcharge for international students but that fee is still less than 500 British pounds per year of study, at least at the time of this writing.

***

The reduction of right and wrong to solely the regulation of our individual lives creates a twisted version of Christianity that seeks to overregulate holiness on the one hand, and completely ignores systemic and societal ills on the other. My own personal sins affect my life, sure. But they also affect my family, and my circle of friends. And the systems which I uphold if I remain silent about injustice reach far beyond my personal circle. All of us uphold these systems if we remain silent about injustice. There really is no such thing as merely "personal" sin, and any gospel that doesn't preach that, isn't the gospel at all.

On a communal level, we bear the responsibility not to let the systems and history we were handed continue. We have the country we have today because of the genocide of the indigenous nations and the enslavement of millions of Africans forced to build our original infrastructure and institutions. Am I directly responsible for any of that? No, it was done before my time. However, the systems that allowed those atrocities to take place were written into the DNA of our country, and have only been somewhat modified with time. Am I directly responsible for the ongoing injustice if I stay silent? Yes. All of us are. We all have a responsibility to do whatever we can to contribute to increasing justice and the thriving of our fellow humans of all descriptions. Otherwise, we have a dead faith in a God that might as well have stayed dead if we truly believe that Jesus' work on the cross was only about our individual sins and our individual salvation.

In *Native*, Kaitlin Curtice writes, "So today, my spiritual liberation is tied up with the spiritual liberation of all my relatives who face oppression, whose bodies are policed and told that they are less than— are we not working to be liberated together, and are our spirits not bound together to fight institutional injustices that have existed in America since its beginning?"[4] When we do not fight for the liberation of others, we not only contribute to the systems of injustice, but we also chain ourselves. None of us are free until all of us are free is a common rallying cry in the movement for systemic justice, and it's true. If I fight for the thriving of everyone, I too get to thrive. And what does it say about those content to be the ones who manage to thrive in this world when they are in the extreme minority? We idolize the rich as though they somehow have more merit than the poor when it's the poor that Jesus blessed and called worthy while observing that the riches of the rich people created obstacles between them and salvation. How did we get it so backwards and inside out?

***

---

[4] Kaitlin Curtice, *Native*, 156-7

There's a sort of thought experiment in white American Christianity that goes, "If you were the only person on the planet, Jesus would still have died to save you." From a standpoint of a declaration of God's love for each of us, it's fine; but it's often used to prop up the individualistic, Jesus-is-my-personal-savior argument. This "personal Savior" language sounds like I'm about to whip" snack-sized Jesus out of my pocket and share him with you like a bag of chips. What a tiny, tidy, easily managed Savior if he can just be my personal one. Just the right number of calories and intervention so as not to make too big an impact in my life."[5]

It's of course a nonsense argument from the standpoint of that's simply not reality. We aren't alone on this planet. And I think the odds of sinning are far greater because of that. All by myself, I suppose I could sin against creation, but creation doesn't provoke me the way my fellow humans do. There's no other way to slice it: we're in this together and we can only move to a better place for all of us to live if we come together.

The late archbishop Desmond Tutu once said, "My humanity is bound up in yours, for we can only be human together." Talking about personal saviors is nonsensical because we are connected—interconnected—whether we acknowledge it or not. We are in this together, for better or for worse; and if we want to work for our mutual thriving, we need to reconnect with each others' stories. We need to take a pilgrimage through experiences other than our own, and understand how so many people are negatively impacted by the systems of our world. Only then can we work together to create systems where everyone can thrive.

---

[5] Anna Elisabeth Howard, "Things Done and Left Undone: the Confession as a Call to Right Relationship."

Numbers

I tell you this
to break your heart,
by which I mean only
that it break and never close again
to the rest of the world.
–Mary Oliver, *Devotions*, p. 146

9

Broken

I dreamed one night that I'd woken up very early from somewhere I was staying with my family, and I'd walked up into the hills across a four-lane divided road. I found an empty campsite where someone had built a fire ring and left several branches burning. I pushed the burning ends into the sandy soil to put them out. Then feeling suddenly guilty for having walked off by myself, I went to cross the road again only now it was really busy and all the cars were going too fast. I stared, frightened, at the traffic, not sure how to get across. I finally spotted a break and ran. And that's when I saw the other women, an untold number stretching up and down the road on either side of me, all of us running to get by the cars that wouldn't stop for us, our bare feet slapping the unforgiving asphalt as we sought the shelter of the other side.

I woke up remembering every solo hike I've taken where I felt guilty for at least a little while because I wasn't with my husband and kids, and I thought it was telling that in my dream all the people dashing from the wild mountains back to civilization across this unforgiving road were women.

When I was a kid, my family used to drive up into the Blue Ridge Mountains in Virginia and do short day hikes off of Skyline drive. I remember the first time one of them crossed the Appalachian Trail and I asked what the AT marker and the white blazes were. My dad explained that this trail stretched from Georgia to Maine and you could hike the whole way. I stood there at the trail crossing staring first one way and then the other, feeling the trail beneath my feet as though it was a pulsing, living thing. I remember staring at thru-hikers with curiosity the next time I ran across some, though I don't remember ever talking to them. I just remember thinking someday I was going to walk the whole thing.

Somewhere between that little girl standing at the crossroad between Georgia and Maine, I forgot my wild. I began to believe the things other people said about me. I was diagnosed with asthma and the same dad who introduced me to hiking and the Appalachian Trail told me in no uncertain terms that I couldn't climb Pikes Peak with a group of friends in my teens because I'd never make it. No ideas about how to train so I could do it next time, in his eyes, I would never be healthy enough to climb a mountain. Which, considering that I'd been on a swim team, was a martial artist, and every winter went downhill skiing on moderate to difficult slopes was a strange place to land, but part of me believed it even as part of me resolved to one day prove him wrong. He couldn't see that I was already an athlete, and I was yet to learn that part of fully seeing ourselves is discarding the negative visions of us that some other people have.

They say total life transformations can't begin on social media; and the anti-capitalist in me doesn't want to admit that a targeted ad while scrolling Facebook woke something up in me; but on the other hand, I'm here to tell the truth, and the truth is, that's what happened. It was just after Christmas of 2020, and I saw an ad from a company I had bought one pair of shoes from previously. But this ad was for their hiking boots, and I thought to myself, "I want to be the kind of person that needs to wear hiking boots."

I'm not trying to argue that an ad or a new product can actually change your life. Though an ad was the sort of inciting moment here, what happened was I felt a pull in my gut, a knowing if you will, that I needed to get outdoors. The irony is my husband had been saying he wanted to hike more for years, and a good friend of mine has been hiking and camping with her kids for at least 20 years, and I'd told both of them, "no thanks, that's not me" to multiple invitations in the past. I guess that goes to show you no matter how old you are, you should try something before deciding you don't like it.

We can't lose sight of the importance of telling the truth about ourselves to ourselves. The question of who we want to be when we grow up is one that we are always in the process of answering, I think.

But telling the truth to ourselves about ourselves is the basic building block of our relationships with everyone else.

***

My mother tells a story of losing me in the house when I was about 3 years old. After searching frantically for me, she found me waist deep in the pond in our backyard, a pond that was rusty-red in color, so much so that it stained my clothes. I picture myself: thin, blonde hair plastered to my head, back to my house, wading into the unknown. What called me to leave? Or what drove me away before I realized I could go no deeper? Was this adventurous child's play or an attempt to escape? Either way, I'm pretty certain I was punished, and a little bit of my wild was hidden away.

That house was situated in a grove of Sitka spruces, trees that must have imprinted on my young mind even though we moved before my fourth birthday. About six years ago, I was searching for a tattoo idea. I knew two things, I wanted it to be about reclaiming my story so I could write the ending, and I wanted it to be a tall pine or redwood style tree. But I couldn't figure out why those two things seemed to work. While continuing my search, I saw a redwood style tree tattoo but it was labeled Sitka spruce. Sitka, I thought. That's in Alaska.

I'd forgotten the state tree of my birth with my conscious mind, but the connection was still there, waiting to be unearthed. I google-mapped the address and discovered that those trees were all around the area at that extremely formative time. Seeing those trees sheltering the place I could barely remember, I felt like a part of myself woke back up. Something I didn't know I'd lost was found, and it was found because I had followed a gut feeling about a meaning behind a tattoo until it made sense. This helped me trust my knowing just that much more: trust that this child of God was trust-worthy, trust that God's image in me was bright and unmarred and–despite the attempts of others–it was wild.

***

I wrote fiction as a teenager. One story was set on a hike of Pikes Peak in Colorado, another set on a hike of Machu Picchu in Peru. I can't remember if that story was before or after I was told I could never hike it myself. Was I writing to appease the thwarted wanderlust? For years I'd already used other people's writings as both escape and adventure. Was I now writing my own escapes?

Before that we lived in the country for three years, on a twelve acre plot that consisted of three fields divided by tree lines. There were numerous outdoor rooms that form the bulk of my memories from this time. The shadowy pine grove with a soft, spongy carpet of pine needles and a slightly spooky feel to it if you sat there as it was getting dark.

We made trails and hidden rooms in the long field grasses, careful to part the grasses at the entrance so as to disguise our secret paths, then trodding down the parts to walk into the round-ish spaces where we played and lay by the hour. I was heartbroken when we moved away. I went to each beloved place and sketched it in a little sketchbook so I would remember it forever. To this day, I can picture each favorite hideaway exactly as it was back then, sketched forever in my mind.

From the Sitka Spruces of my birthplace, to the hideaways on that Virginia property, to brief stints in wooded campgrounds in an RV, an apartment with a tiny bit of woods right behind it that lead to path around a lake, to stately pines above a rental house in Colorado, when I think of "home" I think of trees. It's taken me a while to get back to my literal roots. Coming from a broken family, having been called broken, having my wild chipped away at until I no longer recognized it, I realized that what I associate with home and safety is in fact the woods.

As I spent the last year venturing out more and more and spending more nights outside, I realized I felt very safe overall. I once likened it to a fish in its niche in a coral reef: a statement my friend Shari laughed and took in stride, "sure, you're a fish in the woods, go on." Perhaps a better analogy is a squirrel in its particular nest or hole in a tree, but I think you catch my drift.

This question of belonging hit home while watching a sappy Christmas movie as I worked on some decorations one day. In the movie, this writer, trying to recalibrate herself, visits a tiny village in

Scotland where her father was from before he'd moved to New York as a boy. When she tells the knitting circle who her father was, one woman remembered going to school with him and started telling stories from their school days. The main character begins to cry and says she doesn't know why she's crying. The older lady pats her arm and says, "That's because you've found home. You're one of us."

At that, I began to cry because I feel like there's nowhere that that's true for me. And then it hit me. My home is in the forest, and my ancestors are the trees. Why not? They support all life on earth, and we damage them to our own peril.

I was drawn to the particular piece of land where my husband and I built our home because of the trees. I've since learned many of their names. There's the tall shag-bark hickories that give us edible treats in the fall. Same with the small grove of black walnuts at the bottom of the hill if we expend the work to extract the nut from the pithy protective outer layer. There's stately beeches, lending pale brown leaves all winter in the understory, hanging on to them until the fresh spring ones push them aside. There's the winged elm in the front of the house named Rowena that is one of my closest friends. When she developed some spots indicative of Dutch elm disease, I sobbed until I learned that as a winged elm, she would be able to survive it. There's a couple young showy maples that wait till late fall to really turn colors and then blaze out bright orange to make sure we see them.

***

Perhaps it seems facetious to call the woods my ancestors, but I believe that true family should be the ones that make you whole, not the ones who break you. Of course, as humans, we're all a little broken because we can't get through this world unscathed. And sometimes we act out of that brokenness instead of the healing and we can contribute to the breaking of others. But overall, we should contribute more healing than breaking, more wholeness than fragments. And we do that by embracing the whole of ourselves.

The winter and spring I was finishing up this manuscript, I also decided to train for a hiking marathon. I hiked for the Alabama chapter of Make-A-Wish, helping raise money to grant wishes for sick kids. I felt like having a goal to train for would be personally helpful, and it was a way to help kids with something I was good at doing. My friend Amy called it co-flourishing. After the event, I was talking to Hannah, the friend who got me into it in the first place, and she mentioned how so many of the people who participated had gone through some really terrible things and this was their way of helping, and I thought, they transformed their trauma and transmitted their own healing so that others could heal.

No longer are wishes just for kids with terminal illness, Make-A-Wish grants wishes to kids with serious or chronic diagnoses, and the wishes help give hope to them and to their families. Many wish kids say that the wish helped them recover. So this event in a nutshell shows the power of metabolizing trauma as Resmaa Menakem calls it[1] so that we can contribute to the healing of those around us.

We can't metabolize our trauma without processing it, and we can't process it without getting back into the mess of it all. I remember once crying to my husband as I went around another layer of things I was remembering from my past, saying I was so tired of trying to process all the bad things: I just wanted to be free of it. Freedom lay on the other side of processing, not that I'm completely finished as I don't think such a place exists, but getting to a place where the past wasn't a constant weight took a lot of work and tears. It was completely worth confronting everything from things that had happened to me that I couldn't control, to things I used to believe about myself, to things I used to believe that turned out to be toxic and twisted and harmful.

I once had terrible words hurled at me by someone close to me because I wanted certain boundaries in the relationship honored. They told me I was bent and broken because I wouldn't relate to them on their terms. And the crazy thing was that as much as I rejected their assessment of me, I also believed it. I have always believed it. Or at least, I always used to. Deep down I've been convinced that no one actually likes me, they just tolerate me, and they're just too nice to tell me.

Of course, this fits in and stems at least partly from a very strict view of human sinfulnesses as preached in fundamentalist and evangelical churches. And as people come out of that view, I see the

---
[1] Resmaa Menakem, *My Grandmother's Hands*, 20.

positive affirmation, "I am not broken!" I have made that statement myself, except that it's not entirely true. See the thing is, I am broken. I'm just not fundamentally more broken than you are or anyone else is. I think all of humanity is broken. Look around. Everything is not okay. And yet in the midst of seeing terrible and horrendous things done by humans, you also can find beautiful and amazing things.

Like most things, I don't think there is an either or. I think brokenness and health are inside us and we choose which one to live into. If we don't live with intention, it's easy to end up more broken than healthy. There are many facets of our society that will try to put us into narrow little boxes where we can only exist as shadows of ourselves. This taming, this losing of our wild, breaks our identity and can keep us from knowing ourselves fully. Choosing to rediscover our wild—whatever that looks like for each of us—is choosing to reacquaint ourselves with the selves that had been subdued. This helps us recover and become healthy once more. If we choose health for ourselves and others, we can end up more healthy than broken. The truth is the line of good and evil runs through our own hearts,[2] it's not an external dividing force between groups of humans.

Glennon Doyle ends one podcast with a song by her daughter that has a line in the chorus that goes, "To be loved we need to be known, we'll finally find our way back home"[3] and the line got me thinking. To be loved we need to be known, but how can we let other people know us when we don't know ourselves? How do we love other people as complex, broken, amazing individuals if we don't see ourselves as complex, broken, and amazing individuals?

***

Madeleine L'Engle has a particular gift for this in how she writes her characters. One year a couple years back, I somehow came up with the idea that my Lenten discipline was going to be to read as much Madeleine L'Engle as I could between Ash Wednesday and Easter. I didn't have a concrete reason why I felt like this, I just followed my gut. And by Easter I realized if I could accept her complex, broken

---

2 Alexander Solzhenitsyn, *The Gulag Archipelago*, 168.
3 Tish Melton "We Can Do Hard Things" 2021

characters and extend them grace and understanding, then I could do the same for myself.

I had loved or tried to love other people on command. Believing that the Bible instructed me to love others and being raised in a culture where I wasn't allowed to love myself because that was prideful, I attempted to love others without loving myself. And while sometimes I think love of others leads to love of self, I think if we aren't open to loving ourselves, we cannot truly be open to loving others.

This is still difficult at times, but I think it's the key to moving forward.

***

When I was twenty-five I moved to Tennessee because I'd gotten a full-time youth ministry position and I wanted to be closer to my then fiance. Parts of this time are a blur because there were just so many things going on. Thanks to a financial boost in the form of part of my inheritance from my grandparents, I was able to do some remodeling of an early twentieth-century bungalow in the small town of Winchester. I became an Episcopalian, was confirmed that year, was planning our wedding, and was dealing with a workaholic boss in addition to a fair amount of family drama.

I was working at a church that had designs on leaving the Episcopal church as a whole over the consecration of a publicly gay bishop about two years prior. There were several churches making similar rumbles around this time, and I was only a few years out of seminary and that first undoing and remaking of my faith.

While solidly in the space of loving and respecting all humans—I taught my youth group kids not to use homophobic and ableist slurs—I still believed, because I thought I had to, that same-sex relationships weren't living up to God's ideal. In fact, in at least one conversation, I likened it to a sexual addiction, a comparison which now makes me cringe. I was talking to the parent of one of the teens at the time, and that person had been making some vile remarks about gay people as though they basically were predatory monsters, so my comparison was an attempt to re-humanize the disparaged population for her, but I still believed it was a sin.

And while I would much rather not be telling you any of this, I believe that we must remember our own journeys in order to have patience for the journeys of others. Also, I believe that finding love for our previous selves, no matter how misguided, is key to being loving towards others. That goes back to my work from Madeleine L'Engle's books where I realized that I must love myself as a complex, broken human in order to love others.

Lisa Sharon Harper in a social media post prior to the release of *Fortune*, commented on a quote from the book. The quote was, "The core sin of people of European descent has been to claim exclusive right to humanness--and thus the exclusive right to stewardship of the world."[4] She then went on to comment in her post: "... And they committed this sin in the name of God. Here's the great thing about sin: We can choose another way!" I love the straightforwardness of this: when you realize what you believe is wrong, choose another way. Of course it takes a while to realize this at times as we are predisposed to not want to admit when we've been wrong.

I think we need a new spiritual practice of looking as clearly as we can at our past selves and then learning to love them. After all, those past selves might have believed some terrible things, but look at all the work they did to become our present selves that are hopefully more loving and working toward the good of all our planet and all its residents. That doesn't mean we get to gloss over harm just because we're better places now. We need to go and make things right where we can. What that looks like is probably individual to each of us.

***

I perched on a bar stool in front of a small group of adults. I don't remember the specific question I had asked, but I sat in the awkward silence trying to make space for the answers to come. It was day one, session one of a retreat I'd been invited to design, and questions around the idea of what it really meant to be reconciled to God were lingering in the silence and remaining unanswered. I'd called the retreat the "Three Directions of Reconciliation," and I was seriously questioning my abilities to design sessions at that moment. My

---
[4] Lisa Sharon Harper, *Fortune*, 140.

questions fell flat, and in the silence that followed, I wondered what I could do differently. I was sure all the attendees were wondering why I'd been asked to speak at their retreat.

Somehow we muddled through and then the next two sessions: on reconciliation with ourselves and with each other blossomed into wonderful conversations that flowed with no awkwardness. Reflecting back, I feel like that first session wasn't just about the need to build community into the retreat, but rather, we couldn't connect with the concept of being reconciled to God in isolation. Rather, we needed the conversations about reconciliation with ourselves and each other in order to approach the idea of reconciliation with God.

I don't remember ever teaching anything about homosexuality. My concern as a youth minister was for the kids to understand God better and love their fellow humans better. The premise of the retreat I designed was that we must be reconciled to God, ourselves, and each other. I would add the rest of creation to that now, but I'm still pleased with the overall theme. I'm sure I didn't call out various supremacies by name at that point in my life because I'd yet to unpack the ongoing specifics of oppression at that point in my own journey, but the common thread between the work with the youth and those adults then, and the work I'm doing now was that I believed we should work towards the reconciliation and thriving of all.

This is again, more easily said than done. I've likened trauma recovery to an upward spiral staircase: just because you come back around to the pain doesn't mean you aren't making progress. Rather, each iteration hopefully leaves us further along our healing process than the last even if in the midst of the recurrence or the trigger, it doesn't feel that way.

Our personal growth journeys are similar where we may find the same themes coming up again and again calling us to unpack the layers of what we once believed and examine them for both good and harm. I think this is a life-long process, and part of being accountable to ourselves and our communities means we don't pretend like we never believed the harmful things. Otherwise, how do we help others escape that tangled web of lies masquerading as truth? Each of our stories is a map in the wilderness, helping people find a path that leads to a healthier and loving place.

And this map we draw is sometimes for ourselves, back to ourselves. The layers of toxic belief can hide truths about ourselves from ourselves as much as from anyone else. My husband likes to say that we humans are self-justifying machines. I think we are also self-deluding machines. I think we can want to believe certain things so strongly that we build up realities in our own minds around those beliefs that prevent us from seeing all manner of truth, even about ourselves.

***

The lights were off except for the bluish flicker from the television. I don't remember what movie was on, just the feeling of belonging as we cuddled on the couch under a throw blanket. I had developed very strong feelings for this person and I remember thinking, could I be in love with her? And then I immediately squashed those feelings away and refused to look at them again. I convinced myself I couldn't be romantically attracted to women because at that point I still believed that good Christians couldn't be anything but straight. I slammed the closet door in my own face and locked it for a long time.

I was closeted to myself for many years. Because I'm bi-romantic and also demisexual, it was easy to ignore this for a very long time. And because I don't experience sexual attraction like much of the population seems to, it was easy to fool myself and never look it fully in the face. I want to note at this point, I had no concept of non-binary people. If I had to better explain my romantic capability now, I'd have to go with David's explanation from Schitt's Creek, where he explains that "it's the wine, not the label" that he's interested in.

In this case, it was the desire to love others well that eventually led me back to myself. I realized one day, about twelve or thirteen years before this writing, that I didn't want to believe that same-sex attraction or marriage was wrong. Unlike many of my previous belief shifts, this time I just thought, what would happen if I just stopped trying to believe this? I hadn't done the background work, I didn't have a theological basis that I could really explain, I just thought, I want to put this down. So I did. And it felt like this oppressive weight had been lifted off of me. That was some years before I was able to come out to myself, but I think this is how love works. We learn to love ourselves, and it opens the capacity to love others. And then sometimes, when we work to love others, it also gives us back to ourselves.

What greater story do we have to share with the world than the story of our change? The history of how we grew, how we didn't stay stuck, how we learned new things and new ways of being, and how it opened up the world to become a more gracious and loving place? If we deny ourselves this story, we nip the buds of new growth in ourselves and in others. As we've seen over and over when we look at the texts of Scripture, God is in the story with us throughout history, helping humans move more towards justice and equity. You can point to basically any point in the story and look at what God is doing and see how they nudge us into wholeness as individuals and as a community, starting from where we are and moving towards a vision of human thriving that we can't even see in its completion yet.

Broken

No one would leave home until home is a voice in your ear
saying—leave, run, now,
I don't know what I've become
—Warsan Shire, *Bless the Daughter Raised by A Voice in her Head*, p. 25

10

Hurt

The evening air was unseasonably warm for December: warm enough to stand on the screen porch very comfortably making uncomfortable small talk as folks tend to do when they aren't well acquainted. I tried to remain present and listen to the people around me, something I find difficult when the conversation stays at the surface. I was distracted by the night air and the teasingly complex flavors of the French chardonnay in my hand.

The hostess came over with a tray of things to nibble on. "These aren't for you, Anna," she said firmly as she passed the tray to everyone else in the group. The woman at my left looked startled and glanced sideways at me. I wondered if she thought the hostess was being rude, but in fact, this was the first time I'd attempted to eat at someone's house after discovering I'd developed an Alpha-gal allergy from a tick bite. Basically that means I'm now allergic to all meat from mammals and the by-products of meat from mammals.

I had offered to simply bring my own food, but she'd insisted. She checked with me on several things by text prior to the gathering, seeking to understand this allergy and how to keep me safe. I've always hated having a fuss made over me, so this made me profoundly uncomfortable. She had planned pork sliders as the main course, but purchased and cooked a nice piece of salmon just for me. She made sure there were first course nibbles that were safe for me as well, just not that particular tray she'd brought over at that moment.

Far from being rude, she'd spent extra time and energy working to understand a complex new allergy that I was only just beginning to understand myself. And as I sat there that night, eating my perfectly cooked salmon that was just for me, I thought to myself that this hostess was embodying an incarnational lifestyle even over this dinner party. She came alongside me in order to understand what I needed. She cared for me and loved me right where I was. It would be easy to say, oh, I've made an excellent dinner, therefore I provided for my guests. But if one of the guests cannot eat the dinner, then you haven't cared for that specific guest, only guests in the abstract. But this hostess cared for me in particular, loving her neighbor as herself.

***

I've often considered the incarnation and wondered why it was necessary. Surely God's imagination is big enough that God didn't need to actually enter the world in order to identify with us. God's imagination is big enough to dream the universe into existence, to stand outside all that we know and see it all in one instance, to speak and have life come from a word. And yet, God became flesh. Limitless God took on limits, eternal God took on death, spirit took on flesh. Far from sitting impassively outside our realm, power became ultimately vulnerable, born in a stable in a small town, of a small conquered country: the very last place that one would look for a king.

And then the birth announcements went out. Not to the kings or emperors with power over that country, not the rich living in luxury, not even just to the people the baby had been born to, but to shepherds sleeping out in the fields, living with their flocks during that season to watch over the mother sheep in case they needed help birthing their young, and to foreign scholars, seeking wisdom and looking for God.

While our nativity scenes around Christmas time have rendered these characters ubiquitous, I'd like to stop for a moment and put ourselves in the story, and think about just how strange and unprecedented a birth like this is. On the one hand, it wouldn't be so strange if it was just another poor couple, out of luck for the night, bedding down in the stable, and she happens to go into labor. Just another baby born into the world, loved by his parents, but unremarkable in every other way.

Except.

Except this baby was also announced by over-eager heavenly hosts accidentally terrifying shepherds in the middle of the night. Except this baby was announced by a celestial event that caused a group of scholars to begin a year-long journey to find him. Except this baby so threatened a king that his family was forced to flee, becoming refugees in a foreign country in order to keep him safe.

***

I stashed my pack in the car by 10 am, having woken up, prepared a big mug of coffee and meal-replacement shake, packed up camp, and then hiked four miles out of the woods. I'd made good time; and while I needed to get home, I had time to pay a short visit to the waterfall behind the ranger station. I tripped lightly down the many stairs, swinging my water bottle by its loop, and munching a kind bar as my stomach had finally activated that morning. I'd heard some hollering on the way in and wasn't sure of the source. As I neared the falls, I saw three hikers crossing the icy torrent upstream and yelling all the way across.

I sat down and waited. I wanted a bit of peace to listen to the water as it tumbled off a sheer ledge twenty-five feet into the gulf below. I experience great calm by streams, and I wanted a moment to soak in that feeling. When I'm walking or hiking I can think thoughts to completion, something that isn't always—okay, perhaps is rarely—true of my life at home with my kids in this season. But when I sit by a stream or a river, I experience true mental calmness, as though the water carries all my thoughts away, and I can rest.

I stayed perhaps ten to fifteen minutes, enjoying having the falls all to myself, or so it seemed. As it turned out, I wasn't alone. As I stood to walk back up the trail to the parking lot, movement caught my eye. A small puppy crossed the stream straight to me as if I was his intended destination. He sat on my feet and looked up at me, pert black ears folded over large black patches on his face, his white fur speckled with small black spots making him look grayish in color. I was startled, and picked him up, initially thinking he'd slipped his collar, and there must be a hiker on their way. But no such person appeared.

"Oh no, not now," I thought to myself. My last dog had found me in a similar fashion, but I was unprepared at the moment to take on the task of raising a puppy. However, I couldn't leave him out there on his own, and as he had some wounds, several of which appeared infected, I suspected that he'd been dumped. My first thought was to take him to the ranger station, so determined was I that this dog was not coming home with me.

The little guy was heavy on my arm so I decided to put him down and see what happened. He promptly started trotting up the trail in front of me, checking over his shoulder to make sure I was still coming. Upon discovering the ranger station was closed, I carried him across the parking lot to my car, shut him safely inside, and began making phone calls. The rangers couldn't take him, but I left my information in case an owner was forth-coming. I called a half dozen rescues only to discover they were almost all full. I guess there really has been an influx of surrenders of people who discovered that dogs didn't fit into their lifestyle post-quarantine. There was nothing left to do but take him home with me.

This began a five-day saga of puppy care, rotating him with my boxer, Beau, because you should quarantine strays away from your existing dog for ten days. I did discover the person who'd lost him, but he promptly offered to let me keep the dog. I was extremely conflicted at this point, as puppies are genetically engineered to wriggle into your hearts with great expediency, and I was trying to resist this phenomena. Because he was a beagle/blue heeler mix that would have high energy and a tendency to wander and we have yet to put up a fence in our yard, this free puppy was quickly going to cost us several thousand dollars to keep him. In addition to that, my allergies and asthma were deteriorating rapidly. I'm allergic to dogs in general but certain breeds are worse than others. Between these two things, both my husband and I felt like the timing was wrong, even though posting puppy's picture on Facebook resulted in a chorus of "it was meant to be" style comments which didn't help my heart on the matter.

I was messaging people as well as calling rescues because I really didn't want to take him to a rescue. I'd taken him to my vet when they opened on Monday, and he was put on antibiotics for his infected wounds. Monday night I messaged a friend who immediately said she wanted him. In talking on the phone with her, I realized I was very conflicted, and we decided we'd each sleep on it and see how we felt in the morning.

I felt the best thing to do was to rehome him still, and so two days later I found myself handing him over to her with tears in my eyes, because as I said, puppies wriggle into your heart and then they just hang out in there.

What surprised me about this whole story was not the "it was meant to be comments," but the number of people who acted like I'd done the extraordinary by taking this puppy home. Sure it was inconvenient, but I believe in helping the near neighbor whenever it's in my power to do so. In this case, the neighbor was a puppy. It would seem like that would have made it easier for more people to step up and help, but after the second person suggested sainthood was in order for a few days of inconvenience, and sure, a little heartbreak, I wondered just what it says about us as a whole that the act of saving one little neglected dog was viewed by multiple people as so extraordinary.

Are we really so loath to be inconvenienced by our fellow creatures that we can't save the puppies of this world when they cross our path? I'm struck by this because I feel like puppies are literally the lowest bar, the easiest thing to help. I mean, they're adorable, and they adore you nearly instantly. If we can't help them, how are we to help our fellow humans who are much harder to love by any measurement than bright-eyed puppies who climb into your lap and just want to snuggle?

In thinking about this story in light of this chapter, I can only conclude that the incarnation and inconvenience go hand in hand. It couldn't possibly have been the easiest choice for God to become flesh. In fact, inconvenience barely scratches the surface of that undertaking. If we say we want to imitate Christ, leading an embodied existence that contains glimmers of the incarnation for others, then we are going to have to be inconvenienced and more than often, willing to risk more than a little heartbreak. If we are to participate in calling this upside-down world back to a place of thriving and shalom, we must risk inconvenience and everything else that comes along with the work of pulling our society back from the entropy of injustice.

I like the metaphor of entropy in a society. However, I don't intend it to be read as something that just "happens" with no one driving it, because of course there are always people ready to try to twist society to benefit only a few powerful people. To the rest of us, it may seem like society just happens to keep falling away from justice, however, if we are inactive or apathetic in the work of calling society back towards equity, then we are participating in its inevitable slide towards injustice.

In an article I wrote for Earth and Altar, I reflected on the seeming entropy of my kitchen, and how the orderliness can seemingly vanish in moments.[1] However, it's never really just a few moments, it's usually a couple of days, and the entropy emerges generally because we are terrible at doing the dishes every night. If I don't want to see the effect of entropy on my kitchen, I must commit to actually doing the washing up every single evening and resetting the kitchen.

So too in society we must commit to the constant work of resetting, exerting pressure on our culture, or the grimy dishes of injustice will clog the sink, building up slime and general nastiness, and causing a larger and larger barrier to putting things the way they should be. If we are to imitate Christ, we are responsible for our neighbors.

***

In Luke's gospel we find the oft-quoted story of a lawyer who seeks to justify himself. He wants to inherit eternal life. He knows the law, quoting it perfectly to Jesus when asked: Love God, love your neighbor. But in perhaps a typically lawyerly fashion, he's hoping for a loophole. "Who is my neighbor?" he asks. It is this question that prompts the story of the Good Samaritan. Who is my neighbor? The answer is clear: the one you see in need that is within your power to help.

With the advent of world news and the ability to see all sorts of terrible things at any given time happening in the world, I think we get overwhelmed with the scope of things that need tending to. This overwhelm can lead to paralysis where we can't do everything, so we do nothing. After all, what difference will it make? But to a man robbed and beaten, or to a puppy lost in the woods, a little inconvenience can go a long way.

---

[1] Anna Elisabeth Howard, "Seeking Shalom: Moving from Entropy to Equity."

But this doesn't call us to work without rest, burning ourselves out in the truly never ending work of shalom. Rather rest is part of living into a shalom existence ourselves. Jesus got tired of crowds and went away to rest. He went and prayed on his own in gardens and on mountain tops. He healed people, sure, but even he didn't heal everyone, rather he touched those who crossed his path.

In his work on the Sabbath, Abraham Joshua Heschel tackles the idea of six days to do "all your work." He says, "Is it possible for a human being to do all his work in six days? Does not our work always remain incomplete? What the verse means to convey is: Rest on the Sabbath as if all your work were done."[2] I find this interpretation extremely freeing. I would phrase it as: we do what we can. We do what we can in a given week, and then we rest. We do what we can in our lives—even though there will always be "more" we could have done—and then at the end of our lives we rest. We do what we can. If all of us truly lived like this, taking on the inconveniences of embodied existence, we could change the world together.

I joked with a friend the other day that I have an issue with doing things other people tell me I have to do. Even if it was something I wanted to do or was planning to do, I balk as soon as someone else tells me to do it. Getting a publishing agreement for this book slowed down the writing because as soon as I signed it, I had an external deadline, and I stopped writing for several weeks.

Writing is a lot like hiking and both are a lot like working for shalom in the world. It's one thing to dream up an idea for a book, but the book will never be fleshed out and released to the world without a lot of time committed to butt-in-chair wrestling words and ideas into focus. Sometimes ideas flow, and the words pour out of me. Sometimes. Many other times I'm sitting here feeling like I'm extracting one word at a time from my bloodstream and the sentences and paragraphs are a struggle.

On the backpacking trip where I found the puppy, the first day's hike was a lot like this. There was a mile approach that was very easy, and I flew up the trail. Then I descended into the gulf by way of a natural fissure in the rocks known as the great stone door. It's been used for hundreds or perhaps thousands of years by the first people

---

[2] Abraham Joshua Heschel, *The Sabbath*, 32.

of Tennessee as a passage into the gulf on that side that otherwise is rimmed by sheer drop offs. The land is now a state park, and the trail builders have added stone steps through the door to make it more passable for hikers. I descended slowly down these uneven steps, feeling the weight of my pack and history. These stone walls have borne witness to human resilience, survival, and ingenuity, but also to injustice, genocide, and iniquity.

The first peoples that walked this land were violently displaced and then completely removed in an act known as the Trail of Tears. After years of the European settlers encroaching and breaking treaties, the remaining Cherokee, Shawnee, and Choctaw residents were rounded up and forcibly marched out west. Many, perhaps as many as eight thousand,[3] died along the way, and the great stone door fell silent for many years. Descending through the stone walls, I could feel the history around me like echoes on the breeze.

After climbing down all the steps through the stone door and another wooden staircase down the side, I missed the marked trail somehow. I realized this when I took a step and sank knee-deep into leaves and I realized the trail would be more cleared off than this. Fortunately with GPS, it was a simple matter of stopping in my tracks, and following the little arrow back towards the purple line on my phone that denoted the trail. I didn't have far to go to get back on track, but if I hadn't realized my error, stopped, and course corrected, I could have gotten myself into trouble descending a gulf with sheer drops and large boulders.

The trail continued over boulder fields, sometimes marked by blazes on the ground to encourage me that I was in fact climbing over the correct rocks. By the time it flattened out somewhat towards the bottom of the gulf, I was feeling it in my quads. It's supposed to be easier to go downhill, but it's often actually harder on your body, even if you don't end up huffing and puffing like on an uphill. The next few miles were not difficult, the main thing that slowed me down was the views. The last half mile out though was a steep incline up loose rocky footing that took me forever to climb up.

---

[3] Russell Thornton. "Cherokee Population Losses during the Trail of Tears: A New Perspective and a New Estimate."

So it is with writing. Sometimes the stories come so easily and I can put down a few thousand words in a single session. Sometimes I agonize over a few hundred words, trying desperately to escape a slow page or paragraph, but the words just will not come. But if I keep putting one foot in front of the other, one word after the other, I eventually get to the top of gulfs and mountains, and the ends of paragraphs, pages, and chapters.

So it is with the work of justice and shalom. More often than not that feels like an uphill slog all of the time. But each step—no matter how hard won—is progress, and each step adds up. Sometimes it's hard to see until you actually stand on the top and look back. And when the top isn't something that's achievable in any one lifetime, it's something that takes extra dedication. Trusting the top is there, and committing to the work of getting that much closer in our lifetimes, we have to choose to measure each step as a progress.

On a short hike with my kids, we encountered an ancient tree. Partially hollowed out by rot and time, I wondered how long it would continue standing. I knew that when it reached the end of its natural life span it would fall into the woods and decompose. Fallen trees continue the life of the forest by creating rich soil and canopy space to nurture new trees. I leaned into the hollow space for a moment and listened. The tree said, "It's not about accomplishments; it's about your part in the cycle of things."

We do what we can, and then we rest. The work is bigger than we are, and cannot be accomplished alone. Each of us must commit to doing our part, to practice ordinary goodness each day. We must help our near neighbors first, the lost puppies and people that cross our paths, and trust that as we do our part, it promotes bending the moral arc of the universe as Dr. King put it. That arc is ever so long, and it won't bend itself: all of us must contribute to pulling it the way it must go for all of us to thrive.

***

The puppy wrestled my hand as I scrolled my Facebook notices looking for more people to message about giving the puppy a home. I picked up a chew toy and redirected the puppy from play-biting me.

I was unsettled by the praise I was getting for bringing the puppy home with me, and I was reminded of recent refugee crises where far too many people were willing to make excuses for why it wasn't their problem that children were suffering, children were drowning, children were taken from their parents and locked away, possible never to be reunited again, and certainly never to be the same.

The weight of those children was too great for too many and so they were dehumanized, maligned, and reduced to subjects of debate. Too many people couldn't see their children in the eyes of these refugees, couldn't seem to imagine how bad things would have to be in one's home country would have to be to risk what these families risked. As Warsan Shire put it, "no one leaves home unless home is the mouth of a shark... you only leave home when home won't let you stay."[4]

The weight of those children has pulled on me for years now. Watching as they were traumatized, knowing they would struggle with that trauma for a long time after. Children are resilient they say, and while this may be true, children shouldn't have to be resilient. Adults should be making a world where it is safer to be a child, and where taking home an injured and lost puppy is normal.

Because puppies are a low bar. It was much easier to help that little dog than to fix a refugee crisis. The puppy is practice: the rest of the work goes on.

---

[4] Warsan Shire, *Bless the Daughter Raised by a Voice in Her Head*, 25.

Section Three: Fulfillment

We must risk delight. We can do without pleasure, but not delight. Not enjoyment. We must have the subborness to accept our gladness in the ruthless furnace of this world.
—Jack Gilbert, *Collected Poems*, p. 213

11

Sick

"Are you happy?" she asked me. She stood across the room from me encased in her white lab coat, clipboard held between us like a shield. "No," I said, crossing my arms as my own defenses went up, "but I'm pretty sure that's because I feel like crap all the time." She diagnosed me with stomach inflammation related to a particular bacteria and prescribed antibiotics. I went home and continued my research that had caused so much defensiveness on her part in the first place and discovered there are many things that can cause stomach inflammation, and only some of them are caused by bacteria. I didn't fill the prescription. My test for that bacteria came back negative. She didn't follow up, and I never went back.

This was in 2006, I was newly married, working for a workaholic boss in a ministry job that always seemed to eat up more time, and I was exhausted. But not your run of the mill overworked exhaustion. This was chronic fatigue, stomach upset, sleep disturbances, memory loss, weight gain. If I could have just found a doctor to look at my symptoms, they should have seen classic hypothyroidism was eroding my life. Because my numbers kept coming back in the "normal" range, I couldn't get a diagnosis, even though at this point, I was pretty sure that's what was wrong with me.

It would take eight years to be vindicated. I would lose memories of my children's little years, peering desperately at the multitude of photos I took, trying to remember what it felt like. I would have two miscarriages that were likely connected. I would drag myself through life, constantly feeling bad that I wasn't able to do or be what I wanted to do or be. I went from having a near photographic memory to not being able to read books because I couldn't remember what had come before.

I was finally able to start getting the tiny pill that replaced my missing hormones when I was pregnant with my second child. It helped, but it didn't give me back my life, partly because I was never instructed on how to take it. It would be four more years before I would learn I wasn't supposed to drink coffee within a half hour—or preferably—an hour after taking it. Caffeine majorly interfered with absorption. I learned this from my mother-in-law—a retired nurse—who also has hypothyroidism. Most of what I have learned about managing this condition has been from other people with it. We collectively feel our way in the dark and share each discovery with each other because beyond the prescription, there's precious little information forthcoming from the medical professionals. I wonder if it's because this condition is more likely to affect women than men: there's still a huge research gap on women's health issues.

After learning about the issues caffeine could cause, I carefully spaced out my morning pill from my morning coffee and that made a bigger difference than anything else thus far. I got my brain back, I was able to start reading, and I read like a starving person presented with a feast. I began to dabble in writing again, rejoicing in feeling like I finally had my brain back.

My most recent primary care doctor since 2014 was working to try to get my TSH, thyroid-stimulating hormone, under 2 because she thought I'd feel better if it were there. Only this year as I write this, in early 2022, has my TSH finally gotten under 2. I don't think it's a coincidence that as I finally neared the level she thought would help, I was able to start walking and hiking and getting back into the kind of life I wanted to live.

It has only taken fifteen years if you don't count this last one. Fifteen years that spanned the second half of my twenties and all of my thirties. Fifteen years that spanned the first decade of parenting, nearly the whole first decade of my oldest child's life, and the first six years of my second's. Fifteen years of losing time, of weeks on the couch, of whole body pain during flares. Fifteen of sixteen years of my marriage. Fifteen years of "you don't look sick" and "maybe if you just tell yourself to feel better you will" and "have you tried this fill-in-the-blank with some essential oil or pink shake or whatever they were selling" any time I posted on Facebook about it.

    I felt like a fraud for a long time. Sometimes I was okay and could do all the things. Sometimes. Other times I couldn't, and I felt like I could never make plans because I wasn't sure if I'd have to cancel them. Eventually I accepted the fact that a chronic illness is a dynamic disability because it can flare at any time and cause the need for accommodations. Our society has very rigid definitions around disability. It doesn't seem to allow for people who might be able to, say, stand up from their wheelchair to reach something on a shelf, but can't sustain walking through the store. It doesn't make space for the myriad of chronic conditions that are hard to explain, or that can come and go.

***

    This experience with hypothyroidism was not my first, and as it turns out, won't be my last experience dealing with something that was hard to diagnose and hard to explain. When I was around ten or eleven, I developed terrible eczema on my hands and arms. Or at least, I think that's what it was based on occasional outbreaks in adulthood. I remember being excited about a playdate with a possible new friend. We were going to go to the zoo. I was worried that this other kid wouldn't want to play with me because of my hands and arms. They were covered with red, scaly patches that hardly looked like skin. They itched and burned constantly, but not as bad as the burning inside my soul when I saw people looking at them. I can't even remember this kid's name, I just remember her looking at my arms and shrinking back. Or at least, it seemed that way to me. Maybe I was just so conscious of their appearance that I couldn't think of anything else.

    This ailment led me to my first questioning of what I would later learn was called the prosperity gospel. This insidious theology teaches that if you just have enough faith, you will be healthy and wealthy. That lack of wellness or lack of money—the two always seemed to go hand-in-hand—is simply the result of a lack of faith on your part. Earnest child that I was, I believed what I'd been taught. So I thought, the solution is simply to pray about my arms and God will fix them. Raised on a steady diet of missionary stories and tales of the miraculous, I really had no doubt that it was as simple as that.

One night, I snuggled down under the abstract-shaped pastels that adorned the comforter on my bed, moonlight backlighting the matching curtains I was so proud of, and prayed that God would heal my arms as I slept. I woke up feeling like it was Christmas day. I bolted upright in bed, pushed the covers down only to see no change whatsoever. My gut clenched, and my heart fell. What was wrong with me that my prayer hadn't worked? I believed. I prayed. The preachers had made it sound so simple. I couldn't question God, so I questioned myself.

My bare feet shuffled slowly across the dusty rose carpeting that had been pressed on me by my mother. They had told me I had a choice, that I could choose the carpet for my own room, and then when I asked for a pale green that I loved, I was pressured into accepting the dusty rose to complement the dark blue of my brother's room. It had to be a "girl color." I learned I was never lady-like enough. I never defaulted properly to what girls were supposed to do. My inclinations and desires were always "off" to what was expected of me. Was that my sin?

Memory is a funny thing, where certain things like the night I prayed stand out so clearly, and then remembering when and how my hands and arms finally cleared up is lost to the mists of time if you will. I never had an incident as severe or widespread as that again. What triggered it and what kept it from ever returning on that scale are mysteries that will likely remain unsolved.

The shame I was made to feel because of the beliefs that had been pressed on me like that dusty rose carpet weighed on me along with my skin condition. There was the outward embarrassment of not wanting to look different, but there was the underlying question in my mind of whether or not I'd done something to deserve this. After all sin and sickness were linked. If I hadn't sinned and caused my affliction, then it was a sin of omission in that I wasn't believing hard enough for God to actually heal me.

In this view, God becomes a sort of cosmic vending machine that only serves up healing if you pay with correct change. I'm really not sure how this is supposed to live in the same theology that says Jesus wants to be my "personal" Lord and Savior and have a "personal" relationship with me. This pattern of only responding positively after exacting certain behavior sets people up to accept abuse from leaders within the church. Leaders amass power from people desperately wanting God's blessings on their lives, making those people too scared to question the organization because that would be doubting God, and doubting God leads to all sorts of horrible things.

Distill this down the years and we're left with #blessed social media profiles forming a brittle veneer to try to claim God's blessings. Like the panels on a closet door where the mess has been stuffed to avoid the guests seeing the usual state of the house, the saccharine statuses and pictures that only ever show things going well cover the brokenness and dysfunction that is often the normal state of affairs. This theology is big on faking it. Most people never "make it." But in order to be perceived as being in the "right" place with God, no one can ever share their struggles with anyone else. And in a pandemic, well, admitting fear isn't possible, nor is taking any steps to safeguard oneself or one's neighbors. There is no care of neighbor possible in this theology because everyone should be #blessed if they are just living right. Why care for anyone else when it's their own lack of faith or their own sin that leads directly to the bad things happening to them?

It is no coincidence that this pairs really well with toxic capitalism.[1] Toxic capitalism turns people into widgets plugged in to maintain the system, and corporations into people with more rights than actual humans. Toxic capitalism teaches us that people are only worth what they can produce: there is no intrinsic value to a human life. This let leaders gleefully reassure us that it was "only people with prior conditions" that were at risk of dying from Covid. As though those prior conditions were a capital offense. As though the sin that caused the sickness means I and others who fall into this category are worthy of death from Covid or whatever else comes down the pipeline. After all, if we just had enough faith, we would have neither the chronic conditions, nor would we catch Covid.

---

[1] I say "toxic" though I'm no longer certain that isn't redundant when paired with capitalism. In case that's a bridge too far for right now, we'll assume for the purposes of this book that it's only a negative form and that there's still a possibility of a positive version.

Inward Apocalypse: Uncovering a Faith for the Common Good

If you drew a Venn diagram of the white evangelical/fundamentalist Christians infected by the prosperity gospel and the pandemic-deniers and mask-resisters, I suspect it would be nearly a circle. It also explains why they could support Trump despite all of his obvious flaws. There is no nuance in the prosperity gospel, therefore rich equals #blessed. So in spite of Trump's seemingly obvious sins, his wealth declares him to be favored by God. There can be no crack in the facade of faith or the person who admits the doubts will be punished by God either in their finances or in their health. There's no middle ground, no room for mess, and ultimately, no room to live into the complicated existence that is embodied humanness.

***

When I was about eight years old, someone published a book called "88 Reasons Why the Rapture will occur in 1988." I attended an Assemblies of God church at the time, and the pastor at least partially bought into the hype. The author had identified a 3-day window for God to act, and the first day of that window was September 11, 1988. In church that morning, I remember the pastor solemnly noting that it was the first of three days and we could all be raptured at any moment.

I also remember in the weeks leading up to this date, people went on out of control spending sprees, maxing out credit cards and so forth because they were convinced they wouldn't have to pay it back.

If this behavior sounds incongruous and unholy, it is the latter but hardly the former. If you recall my conversation with an acquaintance in chapter four where I was left speechless by his declaration that "It's all gonna burn," the idea that the planet is here to be consumed before the chosen move on to bigger and better things makes those spending sprees make perfect sense. What my childlike faith at the time made me wonder was why all those things were even necessary if we were going on to something so much better.

Experiences like this have stayed with me, and have helped me form the conclusion that what we believe about the next world, the end of times, or eschatology as the theology professors would have it, matters. It matters because it affects how we act in the here and now.

My friend Amy Kenny in her book *My Body is Not a Prayer Request*, has a wonderful discussion of the description of God in Ezekiel where God is sitting on a platform propelled by wheels. She observes this sounds a lot like a wheelchair to her, and continues "...if anyone had bothered to ask me, they would know that when I picture an idyllic world, I picture ramps. How else would my upgraded wheelchair get around?"[2]

That got me thinking about all the assumptions about what our bodies will be like in the new world. It's not something that's actually discussed in Scripture. We get beautiful imagery of no crying and no death, but the actual mechanics of resurrection and descriptions of the here-after are few and far between.

From Jesus' own resurrection, we can conclude that we will be recognizable to each other. Part of the proof of Jesus' identity was the scars from the nails and the wound from where he was stabbed in the side. His resurrected identity was dependent on the scars from before. That leads me to conclude that at least some of our assumptions about resurrection need examining.

When we assume that resurrected bodies will be "perfect" as in no disability, no flaws, etc, we then work backwards into our world and feel that disability is wrong. Tie that to the prosperity gospel and suddenly disability isn't just something to be corrected in the world to come, it's actually sinful because it's a physical manifestation of a lack of faith.

***

So far I've concentrated on my experience with chronic illness, sickness, and other types of physical disability as related to bad theology, but a recent experience as I was working to finish this manuscript made me realize this chapter would be incomplete without digging into mental health and trauma as well.

The more I've worked through experiences of trauma, the less "triggerable" I am, but I imagine that triggers as always will continue to take me by surprise. I've posted several times on Facebook things along the lines of "Your trauma wasn't your fault. Triggers are real,

---
[2] Amy Kenny, *My Body is Not a Prayer Request*, 149..

and they suck, but you are worthy, and you are enough just as you are." Each time I've posted that, it's because I found myself telling myself that at some point. I would also add that cycling through your trigger is normal, and you are not a burden to those around you.

I'm huddled on my couch as I write today, tucked under my biggest, fluffiest blanket, wearing hiking clothes because I can't get warm. I just made myself go to the kitchen for ibuprofen, vitamin B, vitamin D, and electrolytes because all those things help if I'm cold and achy from a thyroid flare.

I popped an electrolyte tablet into my water bottle, and as I watched it fizz, I chuckled to myself that I was playing the super-fun game of, "Am I cold because of thyroid issues or because of a trigger hangover?" Yes, it's a not-so-fun game that fortunately I have played less and less over the past few years.

It took me a while to realize I had a very physical reaction to being triggered. I freeze. I don't mean I stop moving, I mean I start needing to layer blankets. It's as though my body stops producing enough of its own heat. I have come to realize that a sudden onset of shivering in situations where I hadn't undergone a major temperature change for other reasons came with certain behaviors on that part of people with whom I was interacting.

***

It was past one in the morning, and I found myself pulling another blanket off the back of the couch and tucking it around myself. The conversation felt like it was going in circles. Someone I considered a friend and his wife had come over for dinner and we'd had a pleasant evening. My husband had to go to bed in order to make it to an early service the next morning, and this friend had then steered the conversation towards something he and I had briefly talked about earlier and he had claimed he wanted my input on. He was supposedly trying to understand why I could vote for Democrats who supported abortion, and wanted to know the thought process and theological underpinnings of my current understanding about why I now believed it had to stay legal.

I was exhausted, but had originally thought he had good intentions and was just wrestling with the seemingly obvious decision at that point to vote for whoever the Democratic nominee turned out to be in an attempt to remove Trump from office. But when he started to go back around, I realized that one of two things was happening. He had either come into this trying to convince me I was wrong, or he actually did value my opinion, and he wanted me to say I could understand voting for Trump on the basis of the Republican party's supposed "pro-life" stance. I looked him in the eye and told him that if he was looking for me to say it was okay to vote for Trump, he was never going to get that from me, and I needed to go to bed. He finally left, and neither he nor his wife ever initiated wanting to get together again, something I thought was sad given how big a part of our lives they had been for the previous eight or nine years.

Now this wasn't the only incident, things had been a bit rocky for a year or so, but I thought we'd figured things out and were on the mend. These were people close enough that we'd considered putting them on the list of guardians for our children in the event no family was in a position to take care of them. This wasn't a friendship to be lightly discarded, yet after a couple of incidents where I found myself triggered by this person's behavior in similar conversations. Upon attempting to explain the effect he had on me, getting no understanding or apology of the impact he'd had was really the proverbial last straw.

When we say we're friends with someone, when we say we care about them, then finding out something we've done hurts them should matter. I was perplexed and angered in one conversation when I stated, "this hurt my feelings" and he replied, "I don't care." I'm not sure why I tried again after that, since that should at least be a baseline for friendship. I've learned the hard way that not all relationships can be mended nor does reconciliation have to follow forgiveness.[3] Forgiveness is something I can do on my own: reconciliation requires both parties.

***

---

[3] See Miroslav Volf, *Free of Charge: Giving and Forgiving in a Culture Stripped of Grace.*

This incident is just one of several where people—okay, usually men—have pretended to value my opinion on something only to use it as an opportunity to harangue me. Because of toxic patterns in relationships going back to my childhood, this moves from a nuisance to a full trigger at times. Now, one important nuance to this whole pattern is that there are trigger incidents that are caused by people who manage to push that button unknowingly, people who care about me and wouldn't seek to do that intentionally. From a relationship standpoint, that's an interesting one to unpack because I have to extend to myself the validation of my trigger (just as I'm willing to extend that validation to other people), and still separate the strong feelings that produces from the person who triggered them.

Which brings me back to today, and the incident that made me realize there was a part missing from this chapter that needed to be talked about.

In a sermon on Isaiah 43, specifically the "Do not remember the former things, or consider the things of old" bit, a priest who I have enough of a relationship with to know that they would care about the effect this had on me, used a particularly bad example in trying to discuss why one might want to forget the former things. The example was of a young woman trying to recover from sexual assault, and instead of dwelling on the bad memories on her own, she just needed to confront her abuser, forget the bad, and move on.

I will pause to say, it probably wasn't quite that starkly bad as I was beginning to hyperventilate and left service rapidly at this point. But however the exact wording was, it was a stunningly terrible example in that none of that is how trauma works. Forget for a moment how terribly traumatizing it is to try to report a sexual assault and get justice, and add in the necessary kudos for talking about this from the pulpit as it is often ignored, the idea that a trauma survivor chooses to play dark memories and thus can just forget and move on, is so terrible it left me sobbing in the parish hall, trying to catch my breath while several people moved around in the room next to me setting up something—coffee hour maybe—leaving me feeling completely exposed and also isolated and strange. I mean, who doesn't at least check with the crying person to see if there's something that can be done?

Sick

When I could catch my breath, I went outside to calm down. As my family was in the service, I felt like it would be too big of a disruption to my kids to leave all together, so I went back after the sermon had concluded.

Again I find I must pause to distinguish—for myself as much as anyone—that bad theology is traumatizing and has been utilized in the spiritual abuse of many, including myself. It's therefore possible to hear some bad exegesis, and be triggered even when the overall theology of the person causing the trigger is not of the sort that could be misused to abuse people. This is what I mean when I say that it's sort of sticky to distinguish between the trigger and the trigger-er, to validate the reality of the trigger without demonizing the person who caused it. It's messy. And it's very, very human.

Part of what allowed this to occur was incomplete exegesis. Anytime we seek to understand scripture, we must be careful to put the passage we are considering in its context. This particular section culled out by the lectionary is a poetic passage just after the midway point of Isaiah.

Isaiah is a book that was contributed to in at least four distinct sections that don't go in chronological order. Rather it would seem that, while the first part written may very well be attributable to the prophet Isaiah, it seems his disciples and other prophets who followed added their own insights along the way, sometimes interspersing those with the original text. In no way does this take away from the importance of the text, rather it helps us to see into the culture at the time, and how they built upon one person's teaching and insight and integrated it.

It's important to understand that especially for those of us coming from a western perspective. We westerners tend to be more linear in our thinking, and that's something we need to keep in mind when approaching a text as ancient and as eastern as the Bible. Kaitlin Curtice observed this on her Facebook page in response to criticism of her book *Native*. She says, "Story-telling traditions that are born in and continue to grow through non-linear, cyclical stories are this way! And we should embrace it."[4] The "this way" is referring to the fact that

---
[4] Kaitlin B. Curtice Facebook post March 21, 2022.

she would sometimes repeat things throughout her book as she built the story for the reader.

Isaiah 43 is a poetic song or doxology describing the things God will do in the future. If you look at phrases such as "streams in the desert," it is describing a change of such magnitude that it would not have been taken literally. This is poetic language to convey feeling, speaking to the abundance and provision of God.

Another thing to understand in general with prophetic texts is that they were intended to exhort and comfort a specific people in specific circumstances, while speaking of hope for the future. As such they often have what Walter Brueggemann calls a "double meaning:" a historical meaning and doctrinal meaning. He says that "By honoring such 'double meanings' it becomes unnecessary (a) to have 'doctrinal' readings override 'historical' meanings, or (b) conversely, to have 'historical' readings that deny 'doctrinal' meanings." The really key part to this distinction is what he goes on to say: "The text is both options, provided we are thoughtful and critical enough to hold them both."[5]

In other words, the text had a meaning to the people of Israel then, and we can also glean doctrinal meanings for ourselves. In the case of the text carved out by the lectionary: "Do not remember the former things," we find that the context of the former things is actually all the ways in which God has done good things for Israel, and the text here serves as a warning not to make an idol of the way things had been done before. While God is consistent in their intent to bring justice and shalom to God's people, God's "...methods can always be new, and if we make an idol of the methods, we damn the very thing we should be blessing."[6]

Interestingly enough, the preacher on that day briefly referenced this in terms of the description of the Exodus and other deliverance moments, which made the reference to a young woman trapped in her memories seem particularly out of left field as it were. It didn't fit the text, and it seemed to betray an ignorance of how trauma works.

Triggers and intrusive memories are frequently a part of trauma survivors lives. We don't choose this. We learn slowly but surely to

---
[5] Walter Brueggemann, *An Introduction to the Old Testament*, 174..
[6] John N. Oswalt, *The Book of Isaiah: Chapters 40-66*, 155.

overcome them, and to cycle through them so that in time it becomes less and less intrusive. Unless, of course, there is another traumatic event. All women have been on the receiving end of some kind of sexual harassment. One in five women have been the victims of rape in the United States, and one in thirty-eight men.[7] In both cases, it is likely that this is under-reported, and only quantifies rape. If you expand to other sexual assaults to include unwanted touching and so forth, there are many, many more.

Add onto that the cultural assumption that the victim if female is at fault somehow: "What were you wearing?" and "Had you been drinking?" and you realize that the reason these are underreported is that it often does no good, and further traumatizes the victim. Cultural expectations around masculinity also prevent men from coming forward with their own assaults because being a victim isn't manly, so many just never talk about it and therefore can never process the trauma.

***

When I was a teenager attending a youth group at an evangelical mega church, there was a young man with intellectual delays. He was in his twenties, but attended the high school youth group. He was very enthusiastic and loved to hug people. One night, he was in the same row as I was, and the girl next to me who was an acquaintance of mine was in between me and him. She asked if she could switch with me because "he hangs on me, and I just had a bad... yeah, I can't handle it."

I promptly switched places with her. I talked to her a little more after and decided that our youth minister needed to do something about this. I managed to get him alone after the service, and I explained that this young man was overly affectionate and it was bothering some of the girls. I left the specifics of this one person's story out. He told me I should talk to him.

So at sixteen, I found a way to tell this guy, who was by no means attempting anything sexual or inappropriate from what I'd experienced or seen, that while it was nice that he wanted to give hugs

---
7 CDC

to people, not everyone wanted hugs all the time, and asked him if he could ask people first. He immediately started doing this. The next week, he greeted me with a big smile, and then stopped and asked if he could hug me instead of just doing it.

Even though I hadn't drawn an explicit picture for my youth minister as to why this person's behavior was bothersome, I'd said enough that he should have been willing to help. While it's generally a good practice to encourage people with a problem to talk directly to the person they have a problem with, when women or girls are looking for support from people in authority to deal with men who are making them uncomfortable, the default answer shouldn't be, "well, you go do it." In this case, the young man wasn't the problem, but in other scenarios, being told to handle it myself could have put me in a difficult or dangerous situation.

***

All of this points to the importance of trauma-informed theology and practice. And it calls us to a careful handling of these ancient texts that form the foundation for our practice as Christians. If we don't put each passage back into its context before seeking to understand it, we risk practicing an extractive theology that pulls sound bites of text that we can bend to our wills and shape God in our image.

These sound bites become an incomplete foundation: a foundation that crumbles on examination. But the building built on it continues to offer a facade of safety only to hurt so many of the people who try to shelter within it.

When a large tornado came through downtown Nashville in early 2020, a friend of mine posted a picture of two houses that had been built on her street. These were new construction, "tall-and-skinnies," but when the tornado hit their street, these houses collapsed. The second stories sat crookedly on the splintered remains of what had been the first floors. If anyone had been living in them, they wouldn't have survived. Her much older house next door was damaged beyond repair, but had maintained enough structural integrity to save her and her husband from the storm.

When we build a theology on sound bites and assumptions of how we think things will be in the new earth, we create a structure that won't stand the test nor the proverbial storms of life. Some of us have been lucky enough to escape while some have been crushed as the houses collapsed around them.

Presumably, the materials used to build those houses were similar to materials used to build other houses. Much of it may have even been the same, but somewhere in the design and execution, something went terribly wrong. It doesn't mean the studs or the nails were at fault, but the house that was built with them was deadly. I imagine picking through the wreckage of those houses looking for usable material and discovering there was some good building materials throughout. So too have I picked through the wreckage of my faith. I discovered that not every piece was bad, rather it was the design and execution of the white American Christianity I was raised with that collapsed on me when I examined it, injuring me and many others as well.

Flowers that bloom in the garden are called flowers and flowers that bloom in the vacant lot are called weeds.
—Margaret Renkl, *Late Migrations*, p. 35

12

Other

Standing on the worn wooden floor of the church, I lowered my mask to catch a whiff of the scent I remembered. It's a combination of nineteenth-century building essence and collected incense, and it makes me feel all warm and cozy inside. The priest was celebrating the Eucharist, the words playing in my head as she said them at the altar, and then pitched it over to the congregation for the Lord's Prayer. On cue we all chimed in, "Our Father, who art in heaven, hallowed be thy name. Thy kingdom come..."

I repeated the words from memory as I imagine most regular church goers could, but as I sneaked a peek around me, I saw most people bent over their bulletins reading the words of the service from the leaflet. Thy kingdom come.

I love that the Episcopal liturgy allows you to follow it and be lost in it and be carried by it. On the days when I can't remember how to pray on my own, these words scoop me up and carry me with them until I remember how to find the words again. The liturgy models for us what we need to do for each other. Sometimes I hold the faith for others when they can't believe for themselves. Sometimes they hold it for me. Thy kingdom come.

I love going back to church, especially after so long not attending in person during the pandemic. Yet in this beautiful space with its Neo-Gothic architecture, stained glass, candles, and incense, I experience only part of what I consider church. The experience of church, of "fellowship" if you will, has almost always happened outside of the congregation I belong to. And it makes me wonder, what is really happening in the hearts and minds of my fellow worshipers, heads bent over printed service leaflets clutched in both hands? Are the words of liturgy like water from a stream, gradually wearing the rocks of our hearts down and making new pathways for life to flow? Or are they something we've been exposed to so many times that we've built up a tolerance to them? Does familiarity breed contempt? Or does repetition lead to fluency? Thy kingdom come.

When the rioters stormed the capitol in the name of Jesus and a gospel that led them to proclaim they were in the right despite having decried the peaceful protests against police brutality all the previous year, what were they trying to accomplish? They tried to overthrow a government based on a lie: a lie that was based on so many lies that originate all the way back to the founding of the nation they said they believed in. Based on a fear of immigrants and refugees, a fear of dwindling influence and power, convinced of their own superiority, these people inflicted pain and even death as they stampeded inside, and then stopped to pray out loud. Thy kingdom come?

When the pandemic started in early 2020, people rushed to the stores and purchased up all the toilet paper among other things. While the trend started many jokes, it made me wonder what it says about us as a nation that people's first instinct is to grab what they can and lock it away. And this went beyond just grabbing what was needed, people were stockpiling with no regard for the neighbors in far too many cases. This happens on a smaller scale every time snow is predicted in the south. Everyone runs to the store and buys up all the milk and bread. You can tell what the forecast is on any given winter day simply by checking the contents of the dairy section and the bread aisle. Now granted, we are terrible about actually clearing roads quickly because snow is so infrequent here, but it's also rare that we get stuck for more than a day or so. It always makes me wonder why folks thought their regular shopping was insufficient to last them through the storm.

On the other hand, during the massive flood of 2010, and the tornadoes that came through several middle Tennessee towns in early 2020, I've seen people leap into action to help their neighbors, rally together to support each other, raise money, collect food and necessities, and spend hours cutting tree branches and tarping roofs and so on. But even that feel-good energy was marred during the tornado when the predominantly Black north Nashville neighborhood received no news coverage, and the help was at least initially not being spread evenly across the damaged parts of the city. Volunteer community organizers helped to rectify that difference, but the official channels of news and help moved much more slowly.

What do we imagine when we pray, "thy kingdom come?" We are forever crafting an image of God that is really just an image of us. When we grab what we can because we believe in scarcity instead of abundance. When we neglect neighbors because they don't look like us, or respond to refugee crises based on the skin-tone of those in need. When we allow systems of supremacies to remain because we are scared that removing them will take away even the scraps of benefits we receive from them. It's the toilet paper and bread and milk all over again. We've been taught by those in power that there's not enough to go around, and when there's not enough to go around, people get clannish. They start defining who is in and who is other. Who is human and who is... less. Thy kingdom come.

As I'm working on this chapter, we're getting ready for a local election. I just received a flier from one of the candidates with the name of our county in big bold letters followed by the word "First." In an obvious extension of "America First" rhetoric to appeal to certain voters, this candidate shrunk the base of who we're putting first from 330 million to less than 200,000. What's next? Only my town first? Only my church first? Only my family first? Only me? And how long before whatever we put first becomes "only," and there is no second?

***

At the adventure science center nearby, there's a water table meant to represent the circulatory system. I'm not sure how many kids playing there are thinking about the veins and arteries, cholesterol and platelets, but it's always an attraction regardless. On a recent trip as I write this, the adventure science center was crowded, and there were more kids than usual including several bus-loads of older students there on a field trip. Four middle-school-aged girls had circled the very top of the water table and were damming the water all the way across the top with the little plastic walls. Around the rest of the table downstream were kids of assorted ages, all much younger than the girls at the top. I could see the younger kids were getting frustrated.

Because of the way the table is built, if you dam the water across the top, it backs up and drains so that it doesn't overflow the rest of the table. So essentially four kids were blocking the other ten or twelve kids from being able to play with any water. It was so loud, I hesitated to say anything because it was going to be difficult to be understood.

I was relieved when they left, and instantly dismayed when several older folks, including some adults, took their places and started doing the same thing. Frustrated, I leaned over and said, "When you dam the water at the top, no one else can play, so we're not doing this any more." And I physically removed several of the plastic walls and passed them to the toddler next to me. The adults looked at me for a second and then left, and then everyone got to play.

Now, it would have been better to talk to folks and ask them if they realized that they were stopping the water flow and so forth, though with the noise levels I'm not sure how that would have worked, but in hindsight, I wish I had tried.

But as I stepped back from the table and watched the kids play, I thought about how this was basically society in miniature. A few people consolidate all of the resources and everyone else just has to make do. And I think if you talk to those people they would make arguments as to why they need the resources they have, that they are helping people or something. I'm not honestly sure how one justifies sitting on billions of dollars, but going back to my husband's saying: "we humans are self-justifying machines" makes me certain that those individuals have a justification all worked out.

But whatever that justification is, it only works if you believe in scarcity. And most scarcity is manufactured by those very same people because of their hoarding of resources and wealth. They position themselves at the top, and then dam the resources so that everyone downstream has to make do with a trickle.

***

The world much of the Old Testament is written out of is a world of clashing empires and conquering armies. The gods of the nations surrounding Israel are petty and selfish, demanding sacrifice and blood and war. These gods propped up the nations' war-like impulses and sought nothing less than utter vanquishment of foes in their name.

Some of this language bleeds into the Old Testament, with records of battles and conquering armies. It is important to note that this language of vanquishment was often recorded poetically rather than literally as the peoples vanquished continued to exist. This language isn't what's shocking in a text from that context, rather the language of justice and mercy that we find early on is.

The God that the Israelites get to know as Yahweh surprises them time and time again. They think God wants the vanquishment of the surrounding peoples, and they even record commands from God saying to do so. But then we see God having lunch with Abraham and meeting Hagar at the well. We see God setting up standards and rituals for freeing those enslaved and forgiving debt, and we start to see a picture of a very different God than those worshiped around the Israelites throughout the time period that Scripture was being recorded.

There is a consistent thread through Scripture: God reveals God's self, meets people where they are, and leads them towards a more just and equitable way. But the empires and those petty warring gods—gods of endless appetite and acquisition—they are always there too, tempting and pulling away and conquering. We see an endless back and forth throughout the snapshots that are captured in Scripture. God leads the people towards justice and mercy and thriving and abundance, and the empires pull them away.

It seems like following God's way should be a no-brainer: live like this and everyone thrives. Live like this and no one—not even you!—is left out. But the promise of empire is that a few people can achieve power easily, and those few will always try to grab that even if it is at the expense of everyone else.

It's that _____ first mentality that narrows and restricts until what we end up with is everyone for themselves, and no one working together. It's easier for the powerful to grab more power and resources from scattered individuals than from a united group.

Brueggemann calls these gods of empire "static gods" who only serve the interest of those in power, those who "have" rather than those who "have not." He points out "our sociology is predictably derived from, legitimated by, and reflective of our theology."[1] But the God that Scripture reveals to us is a God who has always been on the side of the "have-nots," on the side of the oppressed.

One of my absolutely favorite passages in Scripture is the one where God meets Hagar at the well in the desert.[2] Hagar was an enslaved, foreign, minority female in a culture where men had absolute power. She was at the bottom of the power ladder. She was abused by Abraham who impregnated her without her say, then abused by Sarah who, despite telling Abraham to impregnate Hagar, became jealous that she was pregnant and drove her away.

Hagar ends up pregnant and alone and dying in the desert. All hope is gone. After all, no one is coming to look for a woman, much less one at the bottom of the power structure. But God shows up.

Hagar joins the ranks of Abraham and Isaac and Moses and the prophets and leaders of the nation in speaking to God face-to-face. And she gets to go beyond that. She gives God a name: El Roi, the God who sees. She is the only person in Scripture to name God: this woman society said was of no importance and sent to die of dehydration in the desert.

***

In God's ultimate revelation—the incarnation—God comes to earth via an unmarried woman, is born in a tiny village far from the center of political power of the day, and is raised by a carpenter. Then when it's time to begin his ministry on earth, he collects a handful of people to be his students: fishermen, farmers, tax collectors, and women too, even if they are not named among the official group by those who recorded the story. These were people with very little if any political power in a conquered nation ruled by emissaries from a distant empire. It could not be more clear. The way of Jesus is always going to stand in opposition to the standards of empire.

So the question becomes, if Jesus stands in opposition to empire, who exactly is being worshiped by the white evangelical Christians

---
1 Walter Brueggemann, *Prophetic Imagination*, 8
2 See Anna Elisabeth Howard, "The God Who Sees Me."

that have aligned themselves with the standards of empire? Well, let's look closer.

Does the god of American Christianity agree with those who seek power or side with the oppressed? Does this god support their war or challenge them to find peace? Does this god love their enemies or hate the people they hate?

It doesn't take much work to see that the god worshiped in these contexts bears more resemblance to the "static" gods of the empires around Israel than to the God named by Hagar who welcomed children and loved enemies. The God who hung out with fisherman, tax collectors, sex workers, and others despised and disempowered by society. That God ended up killed by the state of that day for preaching the message of total thriving for all. Total thriving is only a threat to those who know they hold their power and riches at the expense of the "have-nots." God's shalom is good news for the majority and bad news to the one percent.

***

As we've seen now in the last two chapters, the really insidious thing about American Christianity and the prosperity gospel is that it gets people to participate in their own oppression. If you step out of line, the social cost is high. So to prevent paying that cost, people remain lock-step. After all, the only way they might actually end up healthy and wealthy is if they keep the faith with no shadow of doubt. So women continue believing they can't be in power and that they are less than, and everyone keeps propping up the rich because you don't want to be on the bad side of those empire-god has favored. The reality is that the surface-level beliefs associated with white American Christianity today didn't originate where they claim: the connection to scripture is tenuous at best. It's all a smoke-screen for the underlying issues of money, power, and white supremacy.

I'm writing the conclusion to this chapter the week after the leaked Supreme Court decision that indicates they intend to overturn Roe v. Wade. I'm going to have to turn in this manuscript before we know the outcome of all of that, but it reminded me of the fabrication of abortion as an issue.

Inward Apocalypse: Uncovering a Faith for the Common Good

If you listen to these white evangelicals and fundamentalists now, you'd think they were in the streets in 1973 protesting the court's decision and have stood strongly on the "side of life" ever since. But that's not what happened. Abortion didn't become a hot-button issue until over ten years later. What was the driving force behind that? It was another Supreme Court case: Bob Jones v. the United States decided in 1983. The driving issue in that ruling was that religious schools couldn't claim religious tax exemption if they continued to oppose interracial marriages.

The court's finding against Bob Jones University meant that suddenly, they were going to owe a lot more in taxes and back taxes.[3] So on a conference call to discuss the outcome of the Bob Jones decision, leaders of the newly-formed "moral majority" group were workshopping new ideas. Someone threw out abortion, and that's the one that ended up catching on. There was no biblical basis, no long-standing theological tradition behind it: it became the issue because a bunch of white men didn't want their power and money threatened.

As I pointed out earlier, if it was about helping women and babies, then people would be fighting for healthcare and childcare and education and other things that keep women from getting trapped in poverty because they had children. If it was about all people thriving, the conversation would be completely different.

In his book, *All the White Friends I Couldn't Keep,* Andre Henry begins by talking about embracing the apocalypse. Henry reminds readers that John wrote the book of Revelation—*Apokolypsos* in Greek—to "intervene against a troubling rise of flag-waving for the Roman Empire in his community..."[4] People had begun to buy into the myth of the *Pax Romana*, and even some conquered communities were beginning to cheer for their conquerors.

The parallel here is clear to me. Looking back at chapter eleven and the myth built up around rich people in the prosperity gospel teaching, the idea that to be rich equals blessed by God, gives us a particularly toxic mash-up of empire and theology. Who does this teaching benefit? Certainly not the working poor or lower middle class or even middle class folks who follow it. No, it benefits the few

---
3 Sally Steenland ,"The Religious Right Wasn't Created to Battle Abortion."
4 Andre Henry, *All the White Friends I Couldn't Keep*, 8.

in power, and those people will do anything to keep people following these myths because those myths are the source of their power. Enter American empire and its static god who bears no resemblance to the indigenous brown man with scars in his side and holes in his feet walking the earth to show us that it doesn't have to be this way.[5]

---

[5] Andre Henry closes each week's newsletter with that as a sign off, so I couldn't resist.

"What precisely will you grieve for?"

For the river. For myself, my lost joyfulness. For the children who will not know what a river can be—a friend, a companion, a hint of heaven.
—Mary Oliver, *The Selected Poems*, p. 109

13

Extraction

I chugged up the side of Grassy Knob, following my confused boxer dog, Beau, up the trail. There was a hint of light to my right, and I was racing the sun to the top of the mountain. My headlamp illuminated the narrow track for a few feet in front of me: enough to stay on the trail. Not much else was visible when we started.

Imperceptibly, the light from my headlamp became unnecessary. One minute I was using it to see, and the next, the beam had all but disappeared. We reached the top and I threw down my pack, stuffing the headlamp back in the top pocket, and turned to face the east. The December air was chilly, but my body was warm from the brisk climb to the top. Still, the warmth of the sun was welcome as it reached my face. Golden light suffused the air, displacing the bluish darkness, and the temperature began to rise as we watched. There's not many times you can stand still and watch the earth rotate, but sunrise is one dramatic moment when you can stand on a mountain top and be aware that you're riding the rotation of the planet.

On the east coast of the United States and Canada stands one of the oldest mountain ranges in the world. The Appalachians stretch from Alabama through Maine in the United States, and continues on into New Brunswick, Nova Scotia, and Newfoundland in Canada. Once part of the Central Pangean Range, these mountains also comprise the east coast of Greenland, form the mountains across the United Kingdom, run the length of Norway and Sweden, and form the mountain range all along the west coast of Africa from the south end of Morocco through most of Sierra Leone, stopping just short of its southern border with Liberia.

Some have mocked these little mountains, most of which stand less than four thousand feet above sea level. They compare them to the Rockies or the Alps and say they're basically hills. But the Appalachians are ancient. They are the bones of the earth, worn down by the millennia, and reminding us that we are all connected on this blue-green orb we call home. And when you stand on them, even on one as small and insignificant as the one called Grassy Knob that I climbed that day, you can feel it.

We descended the other side of the mountain following the steep, leaf-covered trail through a tunnel of mountain laurel so old the tops of the shrubs were well above our heads. The mountain we just climbed was just one bump in a series, and we soon found ourselves in a valley between ranges. The sun highlighted the mountains across from us as we turned to loop back towards our car. As I walked, I remembered watching an episode of Parts Unknown, Anthony Bourdain's travel show. He did an episode on Appalachia and explored the past connections in some of these backwoods locales. One of the things that struck me is how they used to blow the tops off of these ancient mountains in order to extract the coal inside. With no regard or care, they left the very shape of the mountains changed, streams choked with coal slag, and a wave of pollutants and disease for the people who tried to live there after.

It's a continuing story of displacement and extraction that follows the colonizing instinct. I find it particularly ironic that these were the very same mountains many of these colonizers came from, and they failed to recognize the connection. Rather they saw it as something to be exploited.

***

In chapter four, I told the story of getting my sitka spruce tattoo. I told how I'd had an image in my head of a spruce-style tree and I wanted it to be about embracing my whole story. I wasn't sure how they went together until I saw the words "sitka spruce" together and the dots started to connect. I pulled up the street view of the house where I was born and wept to see that it was surrounded by sitka spruce. As I began to work on this chapter, the story of the Central

EXTRACTION

Pangean range called to me. I felt a familiar tugging akin to one I've felt in these mountains themselves.

About five or six years prior to this writing, I was visiting North Carolina with my husband and kids. We hiked a mile or so into the mountains with my mother-in-law to see Triple Falls. My youngest wasn't even two years old at the time, so he quickly decided he'd had enough, but my then five-year old and I climbed out across the rocks to get in front of the waterfall. We sat there getting drenched in the spray for a good half hour or so, both of us content. I felt a great sense of peace and belonging, like the waterfall was calling to me, telling me where I belonged, telling me hints of what I needed to be doing.

At the time, we'd been considering a move to North Carolina, but the job and timing didn't come together. I'd come back from that hike feeling like I wanted to move there and hike to waterfalls more often. But when we didn't move, I shelved that feeling, and it took me until mid-pandemic to realize that I could hike and find waterfalls all around where I currently live.

Going back earlier than that, when I was dating my now husband, I flew to meet him in Tennessee, and then we drove to North Carolina to meet his family. I experienced a sense of "going home." I had grown up mostly in Virginia, and frequently went up into the mountains as a child. Driving into the mountains felt like home.

Randy Woodley in his book *Becoming Rooted* points out that regardless of our ancestry, all of us are indigenous somewhere. He invites us to embrace the idea of indigenousness and rediscover our relationship with the earth. He says, "Planting your roots in the land in which you live is the only way to restore harmony and balance on Earth."[1] And I think that—if we are open to it—the earth itself will speak to us of both our place and our interconnectedness.

I felt the pull of the mountains, but I didn't think they were connected to me. I had told my husband some months ago that the mountains had gotten to me, and I wanted to stay near them, at least no further away than where I currently live. Family lore had me believe that most of my ancestors were French and German. The stories were scattered and far between. As I began work on this chapter, I read the introduction at a meeting of the global writers' group that Lisa Sharon

---
1 Randy Woodley, *Becoming Rooted*, 3.

Harper began in early 2020. Lisa suggested that as I began to "stitch the mountains back together," I also should look at where my family was in relation to those mountains.

As it happened, my aunt had sent me a good amount of family genealogy from her father's side that had been assembled by my grandmother before she died. I felt drawn to my great-grandmother as I read the pieces of the family story, some familiar and some not. I realized I knew almost nothing about her, and wanted to find out more.

Fortunately, my husband's hobby is genealogy and when he'd exhausted his family line for a while, he started on mine years ago. I knew he had information and I'd scrolled through it before, but having all these generations at my fingertips allowed me to skim for what I was looking for in a matter of hours. The ancestors of great-grandma Martha whose face had drawn me in and left me wondering about her had settled in North Carolina and then spread out from there to Tennessee, Virginia, Maryland, and onward to Indiana and Arkansas. But they were originally mostly from England. I followed each of my great-grandparents' lineages back generations. Three out of four of my great grandmothers trace their ancestry back to England mostly, with some Scottish and Irish ancestors as well. One of my great-grandfathers was likewise of English origin. One of them was French, but his ancestors were among the earliest settlers in Quebec, specifically Montreal, Quebec which is right on the border of New Brunswick. In other words, five out of eight of my great-grandparents trace long ancestral lines to the Central Pangean range. They moved from the mountains of the United Kingdom to the same mountains in the eastern United States. The French ancestors had been living near the same mountain range in Canada since the early seventeenth century.

I once said my ancestors were the trees and have been known to repeat things that streams have said to me. The trees and mountains lead me home, calling me to roots I didn't even understand.

***

Of course, like all human history, mine is complicated. My ancestors have largely been here since the early seventeenth century which means they were some of the original settlers. In one case, I'm fairly certain they helped found the Massachusetts Bay colony. There's reasonable evidence to suggest I'm descended from an early governor of Virginia, and his daughter married a cousin of Martha Washington.

As I skimmed the family names, some of them stood out to me as the subject of a story here, a memory there. Staring at the family tree I wondered about all the lost stories and then wondered also at the ones that made it in. Some of my ancestors are the colonizers that came here and stood on the same mountains they were born in and didn't recognize them. They pushed aside the people who were indigenous here, forgetting their own indigenousness in the process and severing their connection to the land. They participated in the enslaving of people stolen from the southwestern part of the Central Pangean range and didn't see that they all lived on the same land: they didn't see that they were connected.

By dehumanizing some humans, they damaged their own humanity. They explored and exploited. On my shelf sits a record of one of my ancestors—five "greats" back—Gabriel Franchère who explored with John Jacob Astor, pushing the westward expansion of the United States and Canada. Two "greats" back in another line is Andrew Jackson Miller, named clearly for the US president responsible for the Trail of Tears, and yet this person's parents thought he was someone to be emulated.

Among the bits and bobs of memories my grandmother jotted down from my grandfather's family is a story of my great-uncle taking his new model T and driving it across the bridge to scatter families from the Black church gathered for a baptism. He'd done it on purpose, he said, and I guess he was proud of it however many years later because of the scattered recollections and memories, this was one he chose to tell.

I wonder at all the things that weren't told. My great-grandmother on that side died at sixty-three, perhaps not surprising after giving birth to fourteen children, eleven of whom survived. I met most of her children and their spouses, and some of their children at one family reunion for that side of the family.

It was loud and full of constant conversation as the siblings and their spouses reunited and got reacquainted. I had to have been around seven or eight at the time, so everywhere I looked were bellies and belts and shirts. I squeezed through all the bellies and took refuge in the cool, dark basement with the pool table and some of the other kids where the volume of the conversations above receded from a din to a hum.

I was so young that I only recall snippets of this multi-day gathering at my grandparents house. I remember my grandfather's siblings talking about their mother but never their father. I heard whispers about abuse from the father, mostly speculation on the part of the next generation, but my grandmother managed to confirm that in one tiny story where one of my grandfather's brothers remembered an older brother stopping their father from beating him.

My grandfather has always been a man of few words. At the time of this writing he is living, approaching his ninety-ninth year of life, and he no longer remembers who I am. I used to call to talk to them when my grandmother was alive. She would talk, and then I would ask to talk to Grandpa. He'd get on the phone and say, "Tell me a story." Uninterested or perhaps incapable of sharing himself, he never failed to be interested in what I was doing. No matter what I told him, he'd tell me, "That's a good story!" and then pass the phone back to Grandma. I wonder now why he told so few of his own stories, locking away the good and the bad of his life behind a remote exterior. He lived his life and did his duty by his family in terms of financial support, education, and so forth. I never doubted that he loved me, but to this day, I don't feel like I really know him.

My grandfather benefited from the GI Bill that helped him go to college, buy a house, and surpass the economic level he was raised in. On two teachers' salaries, my grandparents managed to always own their home, and for a while owned a vacation home in Florida,. They amassed a small nest egg they then passed on to their four grandchildren. And they gave it to us well before they died so they could see us use it. It's because of this that I was able to build the house my family and I live in today.

But these advantages were passed out unevenly. Only soldiers of European descent got to benefit from them: they were denied to Black soldiers. As a country, we intentionally continued to enforce laws that increased the wealth gap between families of European descent and families of global majority descent.

My grandparents were both children of the Great Depression which made them frugal to the extreme and generous with family at the same time. My grandfather grew up on a farm, so they always had enough to eat, but both of them forsook the closer-to-the-land living as they moved into suburbia and the doctrine of the 50s that said formula was better than breast milk and white bread was more "pure" than whole grain.

I remember staying with them once when I was probably eight or nine years old. When I got hungry, grandma made me a snack that was a piece of American cheese on white bread that she microwaved until it melted. It was floppy and warm and I thought it was a novelty. I sat at the mid-century modern wooden table that had been in their kitchen for as long as I could remember on one of the avocado green chairs that surrounded it. Even when they moved into a new, single level house for their retirement years, that table followed them and stood in the eating area of the new kitchen, looking slightly out of place amid the standard builder-grade beiges and light oaks of the early 21st century.

I wonder if it was the itinerant lifestyle and my grandfather's unwillingness to talk much about his past that led my grandmother to compile what she did about his life and ancestors. They moved all over the country, and even lived abroad for a few years. I wonder if she had been searching for roots. I wonder if she found them.

My grandfather gardened all his life. I have a few plants that he gave me, dug fresh from his garden and sent home with me on a visit where they also gave us a table and chairs they'd acquired at a yard sale and thought we might use. The table is a sturdy oak number that despite the damage wreaked on it by my children when they were young is still in use today. I surrounded it with sturdy rock maple chairs I found at a local antique store and a pine bench that went with a table I used when I was child. I bartered the table and one bench away years ago, but kept the other as a reminder.

My grandmother's antique tea cup collection and Hummel figurines sit in a maple secretary desk from the late 19th or early

20th century that was passed down from the great-grandmother I was named for. Delicately painted flowers adorn each unique cup and stand out—still vibrant—against the muted earth tones of the figurines.

The cabinet itself traveled up the Alcan to Alaska before I was born, and has since moved all the way back to Tennessee and the glass in the upper cabinetry is somehow still intact. That's more than can be said for my family.

I sit here surrounded by physical reminders of all the people that came before me. When researching my ancestors for this chapter I was struck by the number of people that just expands the further you go back and realizing the odds of existence for any one of us is really terribly small. And yet, here we are. Each and every one of us is a miracle of existence who holds a record in our very cells of history and movements of people.

There's a Doctor Who episode with Matt Smith's doctor and he's asking after the well-being of someone, and another character replies they're "nobody important." And the Doctor replies, "In 900 years of time and space, I've never met anybody who wasn't important."[2] The character was a rich tycoon type who was controlling the skies over an entire planet with a weather machine his father had invented. He also kept people in stasis as living collateral for their families debts.

Seeing people as nothing more than some kind of monetary worth tracks perfectly with toxic capitalism trying to turn everyone into widgets. This kind of thinking is really as old as anything as people with power have always seen people with less power as resources to be exploited rather than seeking the thriving of everyone. There has always been enough to go around, and we could always have thrived together, except some of us aren't interested in that at all and continue to extract and exploit wherever the opportunity arises.

Instead of seeing each human being for the miracle they are, some will see only that which can be used. Soldiers to be fodder on the battlefield, the individuals that don't matter as long as the overall numbers work out. Manufacturers to spend their bodies and lives mass-producing items to be sold on the cheap and discarded when they wear out, and the individual producers don't matter as long as

---
2 Doctor Who, "A Christmas Carol," 2010.

not too many are injured or forced to quit. Individuals whose odds of existence are infinitesimally small are forced to trade the miracle of their existence in order to try to continue it, trading health and youth for food and shelter. The corporations we in the United States legislated into people don't care if anyone actually has a good quality of life as long as the corporation has a good bottom line. After all, they are the people now and we, we are the widgets that keep production going.

And somehow the church—particularly the white evangelical/fundamentalist church—has bought this line of reasoning and now it's hard to say what came first: the theology or the practice. In the church, people become numbers to fill a pew, sources of income, and stories to tout as successes. It's ironic. I was raised in this tradition and taught that "it's not a religion, it's a relationship" and "it's not about a bunch of rules to follow." And yet there were so many rules: rules that actually go against love of neighbor and seek to prop up the supremacies of our world with a veneer of theological rationale.

***

Crystal Good's spoken word poem "Boom, Boom" appears in the West Virginia episode of Parts Unknown. It juxtaposes women working as strippers with the tops of the mountains being blown away in order for the coal resources beneath to be strip-mined. She shows the outsiders coming in to exploit the people and the mountains simultaneously.

The coal that built America was pulled from those mountains; and when the companies found cheaper places to get it, they abandoned the communities that had sprung up around the mines. There are still mines, but not on the scale there once was.

As Anthony Bourdain pointed out, "It's easy to say from afar that coal's time here has come and gone, that we should let the miners move, find some other work. What other work? The state's biggest employer is now Walmart."[3] And while there's nothing wrong with working at Walmart, Walmart doesn't pay like the mines do.

---

3 *Parts Unknown*.

Bourdain dined at a farm that specializes in foraged food and heirloom crops. One of the owners pointed out that the food of poverty has become trendy, and things like ramps at the time were selling for upwards of $30 a pound in New York City, while the person who foraged them in West Virginia probably got paid $2 a pound or something like that. Yet another example of extraction at work.

When my ancestors joined those first waves of European settlers in the seventeenth century, many would have considered themselves as fleeing religious oppression. Some probably were just adventurers seeking new opportunities. They arrived in a place already populated, and, convinced of their own superiority, largely sought to subdue the original inhabitants of this continent. One may observe that while this is something that happens throughout human history, it took on a different tone in what would become the United States. After years of forcing the migration of enslaved people from Africa and years of conflict with the indigenous nations of Turtle Island, the European settlers began making laws to define in very strict and narrow terms who had the power. They divided people based on skin color and gender, making it so the children of an enslaved woman were to be enslaved no matter who the father was, and united the various Europeans who before might have viewed each other as foreign: considering that they spoke multiple languages and originated from different, distinct countries.

Thus the idea of "whiteness" as an identity was born and then elevated over the concept of anyone "not white." Many European settlers came here with an idea that God was sending them to a new country. Combine that with some carefully extracted scriptures and you begin to find the theological underpinnings for what would some two hundred or so years later be called Manifest Destiny.

It may have only been named that in the mid nineteenth century, but the idea that light-skinned Europeans were superior and had the right—or even a calling—to go "subdue" the entire continent and the people in it, was one that had its roots right at the beginning of the nation before this was an actual nation.

***

The stories we tell are important. But it is also vital that the stories we tell are not a smokescreen for the stories we don't tell. In the family history that was handed down to me, I was told of connections to historical figures, stories of abolitionists, and one fiery Methodist circuit rider. I heard about my grandfather's boyhood horse, and the death of my grandmother's brother at nineteen. These stories were real, albeit curated. Like all families, mine is a mixed bag and our history is complicated.

Social media gets a bad reputation for allowing people to curate their lives and present only a polished image to the world. But people have been curating their lives for all of time in their oral traditions and photographs. Social media allows us to do that at another level perhaps, but it's nothing new. If anything, it's a magnification of human nature because of the frequency and exposure it allows.

Perhaps it is the ultimate in individualistic self expression: expression that allows us to turn our lives into a brand and try to set ourselves apart. But none of us stand on our own. We are connected to a vast number of ancestors whether we like it or not. There is so much to be learned from discovering who we came from and where we came from. The lessons of history are in our blood, waiting to be discovered if only we take the time to realize that none of us sprang to life fully formed and without connections. None of us came here on our own, and none of us can exist on our own.

Dysfunction I still don't completely understand kept me from knowing my grandparents fully. The more I learn about them, the more I begin to understand the reasons why the life they shared was so carefully curated. Not because they were intentionally covering anything nefarious, but a combination of the expectations of the era they grew up in combined with trauma both personal, national, and global in the form of siblings lost, the Great Depression, and then World War II meant that they lived carefully. They also knew how to have fun, and hang out at the beach with their grandkids and live in the moment.

My grandmother's desire for connection reached back into history and pulled together vital pieces of information that she then left to her daughter, my aunt, who passed them onto me just this year. I looked at the faces of my family and I saw myself. I saw the story that led to my existence and it is a beautiful story, a complicated story, and a sad story all in one. Reconnecting to it gave me a context for the personal work I had been doing, work that until then had been extracted from the backdrop of my personal history. And while not complete, the pieces of my story have begun to make more sense because of better understanding the interconnection of my story with my ancestors.

EXTRACTION

"It's like in the great stories, Mr. Frodo. The ones that really mattered. Full of darkness and danger they were. And sometimes you didn't want to know the end. Because how could the end be happy? How could the world go back to the way it was when so much bad had happened? But in the end, it's only a passing thing, this shadow. Even darkness must pass. A new day will come. And when the sun shines it will shine out the clearer. Those were the stories that stayed with you. That meant something, even if you were too small to understand why. But I think, Mr. Frodo, I do understand. I know now. Folk in those stories had lots of chances of turning back, only they didn't. They kept going, because they were holding on to something. That there is some good in this world, and it's worth fighting for."
—The Two Towers Movie

14

Story

There's a fish tank in the entryway to my house, and the last few weeks have been so consumed with other things that I've let it get low. So the water from the filter has created a waterfall. Instead of smoothly rippling the surface, it now falls four inches to the body of the water as it slowly evaporates down the sides of the tank. The entryway is small, with a stone floor, magnifying the voice of the water ever so much louder than its typical trickle would dictate.

I always wonder if the fish notice when the tank gets like this. Do they think the sky is falling? That their world is shrinking? Or are they just so acclimated to the water, and the evaporation happens so slowly that perhaps they would not notice it until it was almost gone. Do they tell themselves everything is okay? Do they think this is the way things have always been?

Later today I will go fill the tank back up and clean the glass, removing the marks of minerals left behind as the water crawled downward. Replacing the gallons that have evaporated will make their world bigger by 20% or so. It will let the taller plants stand up straight again. They've been stooping ever lower for weeks, reluctant to break through that bead of tension at the surface, preferring to stay submerged for as long as possible.

I wish I could do the same for people.

***

I grew up in a fish tank with water too low. Those in my circle saw things to fear wherever they turned. As they tried to maintain what they thought of as righteousness and purity, their world shrank. Like the plants in my tank, they ended up bowed down, crouched down, afraid to break the surface to the world beyond the waters they knew. And I, like a tiny fish not realizing I was in an evaporating pool, swam on until I could swim no more.

Really, I should put a lid on this tank, to slow evaporation, I'm not sure why I never have. It takes more maintenance this way than my smaller tanks that house my bettas. Those have glass lids by necessity, however. You see, bettas' habitat in the wild are the wide, shallow, slow waters of rice paddies in Vietnam and Thailand. Sometimes they can get caught in smaller pockets of water when water levels are low and finding themselves trapped, they take a leap of faith. These fish jump from their puddles and flop across the mud to find the main water of the paddy again. Of course there's a risk. They may flop the wrong direction and never find the water again. But if they do, they're back in the wide world of the main paddy they'd come from.

Really the risk is minimized if you think about the fact that the puddle could dry up all together. So it's either jump while the water is high enough to get out, and have a chance to join the world; or stay, and risk the water not coming back in time to save you.

I jumped. And yes, I flopped for quite a ways at various times, gasping for air, stuck in the mud, not sure if I would ever find my way back to the waters of the world again. I don't know if it hurts the bettas to do this, but I do know that it hurt me quite a bit.

There were people I loved and cared about back in that puddle that wouldn't jump with me. They are so convinced that the puddle is right, and the smaller it gets, somehow the righter it is. And I've tried to call them back to the main water, the less polluted main body of water, but they are so convinced that this water in the puddle is the purest even as it becomes more and more toxic around them.

I've noticed that the people in the puddle-world have become so convinced their water is the best, they will actively resist you trying to make their puddle bigger or their water less toxic. They will resist to the point of attacking the containers of less toxic water, convinced you are trying to kill them, instead of helping them. That's where fish are superior, I guess. They come to play in the stream of water as I fill the tank.

Story

I was talking to a therapist friend of mine this week about narcissists and how they could technically change if they really, really wanted to. I said that reminded me of Voldemort in the Harry Potter books. He could have put his soul back together, but he'd have had to feel remorse. And that would have been painful, but ultimately worth it. But he didn't even try for remorse, instead, he tried to kill Harry one last time, ultimately succumbing to his own death spell as it backfired on him.[1] I guess the more you give away pieces of your soul, the harder it is to ever come back.

And from where I sit, white folks in this country have divided their collective and individual souls many times at many levels. The main group of these that have been most active are white evangelical Christians. But the puddle of their world, while never particularly expansive, has spent the better part of the last forty-some years shrinking still further.

I sat with the events of the first week of January in 2021, and I remembered Ruby Sales admonition to find a liberation theology for white people,[2] and I struggle to find anything that I could say to them that would make them realize they are killing themselves with weapons of their own making, while trying to kill the rest of us first.

What happened at the Capitol on January 6, 2021 was not a surprise to almost any Black or Indigenous person in this country. This is the America they have always known. This is the America you see more and more as a person of any race that chooses to unpack white supremacy and anti-Black and Indigenous racism. Another friend said of this week that as a white person it was like a red pill, blue pill scenario where once you see it, you can't unsee it. Or another example I saw online likened it to high-fructose corn syrup. Once you know to look for it, you realize how much it's in everything. Once you start unpacking white supremacy and racism, you discover there are seemingly endless layers to peel back, deconstruct, and so many things to discard.

And yes, it's uncomfortable, and it's painful, but isn't it worth it? Because it's the only way to reclaim our souls. The only way to live in harmony with our siblings of all colors. The only way to experience

---

1 J.K. Rowling, *Harry Potter and the Deathly Hallows*, 737-744.
2 Krista Tippet, interview with Ruby Sales.

God's shalom for ourselves and participate in building that world, instead of tearing it down.

I just wish I could convince more of my friends and family of European descent that the work is so very worth it. The struggle in the mud is temporary, and the waters on the other side are so much wider and sweeter than you've ever known. It hurts that the choice to do this work—to make the jump—left so many people I love behind.

I'm reminded of the soldiers at the end of C.S. Lewis's *The Last Battle*.[3] Having been brought into paradise, they were so far from the love of Aslan that they couldn't see it. They experienced it as a dark and nasty place, a place they were stuck in a dirty stable, even though the stable no longer existed. The children tried to give them strawberries, and the soldiers experienced it as the children throwing dung at them. They were forever locked in a hell of their own making, and nothing could be done for them.

But things don't have to go on like this. A new world is possible, and we can all take part if we choose to take the leap leaving the toxic puddle of Christian nationalism and white supremacy behind. For people who tell a story that things will get worse and worse and then Jesus will whisk them all away to a front row seat in the clouds to watch the torture of the heathen, these folks fight so hard to make things line up with their worldview.

***

What's in a story? At the end of chapter 11, I talked about a poor sermon example I heard of a young trauma survivor and how in the preacher's estimation, this would leave her "backed into the corner of every room." And I thought about all the women I know personally who are survivors of various forms of trauma and how they took what was done to them and let it make them kind. Trauma survivors are enormously resilient, not because of the trauma, they were resilient anyway. But when you can point to a trauma survivor who is out here working to make the world a kinder and more just place, you see that they transcended the violence that sought to steal their very identities

---

[3] C.S. Lewis, *The Last Battle*, 746-747.

and transformed their healing process into something that can be transmitted.

It was a trauma survivor in scripture that became the very first apostle: the apostle to the apostles, Mary Magdalene. Nadia Bolz-Weber in her sermon, "While it was still dark" preached at Rachel Held Evans' funeral, pointed out the contrast between what Peter and John saw and what Mary saw. John's gospel[4] has Mary Magdalene discovering the stone has been moved and then running back to tell the gathered disciples what she found. Peter and John come running, with the lovely note from John that he was, in fact, faster and beat Peter to the tomb. Though once there, he gets scared (my interpretation) and waits for Peter before going inside. They go in, and they see Jesus' burial clothes lying by themselves.

Perplexed, they leave, because "...as yet, they did not understand."[5] Mary stays, seeking perhaps through her tears to understand, or so bereft at the loss of the person who had freed her that she couldn't bring herself to leave. She stoops to look inside the tomb, and as Nadia put it, "Because unlike when the men looked in and saw only laundry, when Mary Magdalene looked in the tomb, SHE saw angels."[6]

It does make me wonder. Were the angels there when Peter and John looked in? Nadia implies that it's possible, and I love this. She argues that Mary was chosen not despite who she was, but because of it: "I think Mary was chosen **because** she was a woman from whom demons had fled. I think Mary was chosen, because she knew what it was like for God to move; not when the lilies are already out in church and the lights are on—but while it is still dark."[7]

I think there are hints in the text that support the idea that the angels were there and Peter and John couldn't see them, even if we cannot say for sure. What we can see clearly in the text is that the resurrected Jesus waited until Peter and John were gone and then appeared to Mary Magdalene. Jesus waited. This is not a mistake. He doesn't tell her to run after them and call them back please so he can explain what happened. He knows her best of anyone and he knows that she will be the one who recognizes him the fastest. The trauma

---
[4] John 20:1-18 NRSV
[5] John 20:9a NRSV
[6] Nadia Bolz-Weber, "While it Was Still Dark."
[7] *Ibid.*

survivor, the one who had been freed from so much pain and darkness in her past, the one people spread rumors about later and probably during her life as well: Mary Magdalene was uniquely equipped to see what others couldn't.

At the end of *The Two Towers* movie, the screenwriters adapted a speech from the books that Sam makes to Frodo:

> "It's like in the great stories, Mr. Frodo. The ones that really mattered. Full of darkness and danger they were. And sometimes you didn't want to know the end. Because how could the end be happy? How could the world go back to the way it was when so much bad had happened? But in the end, it's only a passing thing, this shadow. Even darkness must pass. A new day will come. And when the sun shines it will shine out the clearer. Those were the stories that stayed with you. That meant something, even if you were too small to understand why. But I think, Mr. Frodo, I do understand. I know now. Folk in those stories had lots of chances of turning back, only they didn't. They kept going, because they were holding on to something. That there is some good in this world, and it's worth fighting for."[8]

I used to re-watch the *Lord of the Rings* trilogy when I got sick and I identified a lot with Frodo. He endured a lot, while trying to do the right thing. He was an imperfect person who couldn't do what he did without the support of his faithful friend Sam, and many others throughout the story. Ultimately, he tells Sam that they had saved Middle Earth, but they hadn't saved it for him.

Stories of surviving and overcoming wouldn't be complete without realizing there are plenty that don't survive and don't need to be shamed in retrospect. Whenever I'm watching a movie such as one of the *Lord of the Rings* trilogy with sweeping battle scenes and eventually triumphant heroes, I always wonder about all the other soldiers. The ones whose bodies litter the field in the wake of the

---
8 *The Two Towers* Movie

violence: the ones who fought their hardest and gave their all and they still didn't make it. I think of those who died from their mental illness, and know there is no more shame in that than those who died of their cancer.

It's why the metaphors of fighting and battling and beating diseases have always made me uncomfortable. Those who "lose" fought just as hard—if not harder—than the ones who "win." We are all complex, broken, beautiful, unique people. This is where toxic positivity meets the prosperity gospel in our culture. Where even if the language isn't put into terms of faith and belief, there is this pervasive and insidious notion that if you just fight hard enough—believe hard enough—that you can recover from your illness, no matter what it may be. But the people who believe that must never have been at war.

In a battle, you realize that survival is less about skill and more about luck. That explosion that killed your friend and spared you? There's no rhyme nor reason to that. Am I downplaying the strength it takes to survive? That is not my intent, although I have to approach all of this with humility because I can't always judge the impact. I'm attempting to hold up the strength and wisdom of trauma survivors and bear witness to the life they generate out of the things they have learned, and also as a trauma survivor I'm aware that I can't even quantify exactly how I made it through. I've learned to heal, and at least part of that was because of great stories like the ones Sam is referencing in that speech.

The great adventure stories always have darkness, and times when it's so scary you're not sure you want to read to the end. But if we read scripture and look for those trajectories of justice and thriving for everyone, then we can say that no matter how dark it is where you are right now there is a God who will make everything new. And that God who makes everything new invites us to share in the renewal. Not because God needs to "use" us like we are some kind of currency, but because we are created in God's image. We are part of God, and God is part of us and out of that, we can collectively make all things new.

Nadia Bolz-Weber went on to say:

> "Mary Magdalene saw angels because she was not unfamiliar with the darkness. She had the kind of

night vision that only comes from seeing what God does while it is still dark. I do not know why this is God's economy. That it is while we are still in despair. That it is while we are still grieving, while we are still sinners, while we are sure that nothing good will ever come. That it is when we are faced with the nothingness of death—that we are closest to the resurrection. That it is while it is still dark that God does God's most wondrous work."[9]

Telling a story where we work with God to make all things new is a very different story then one where God is going to swoop up the faithful and take them off to party in the sky while those left behind endure all kinds of torment, presumably while the partiers in the sky look on. Telling a story where one is part of the faithful in the sky essentially others all those who are left. Like that acquaintance I referenced with his laconic, "It's all gonna burn" attitude, how does rejoicing in being the faithful while other humans are tormented create anything but an "us versus them" scenario? And if that's what one believes about the end of time, how does that lead one to treat their neighbors now?

* * *

I walked across the campus of the junior college I was attending at the time. I'd started taking classes there at eighteen after moving to California with my family. The sun was hot and was beating down between the squat, square buildings that blocked the near-constant breeze off the ocean just a few miles west of the campus. My palms were sweating, and I had a familiar knot in my stomach: one I always had when I tried to do what I was about to attempt, but I felt like I had to do it anyway. This was before I learned that my femaleness didn't make me less, that my heart was created by God and wasn't wicked and deceitful by default, and that I should trust my knowing.

I saw him standing in the doorway to the classroom, chatting with a few other students. I could never figure out how he'd ended up

---
[9] Nadia Bolz Weber, "While it Was Still Dark."

teaching at a junior college. His trim white goatee and quintessential professors uniform of tweed jacket and bow tie wouldn't have been out of place at much more prestigious schools than this one. And I loved his class. He was very encouraging to me, and I thought the least I could do was make sure he didn't go to hell.

I don't remember exactly what I stammered out, but something along the lines of being concerned for his eternal destiny. He sighed, and we went back and forth for a minute. I remember he asked a few questions. As I responded, he smiled: "So, you're selling me fire insurance then."

I didn't have a good answer. I mumbled something, already feeling embarrassed, and awkwardly exited the situation. He had been very kind given my intrusion, and he left me with a question that would contribute to the erosion of things I thought I had to believe. Of course this also ended up changing or severing a number of supposed friendships, as in the immortal words of John Prine: "I chased a rainbow down a one-way street dead end / And all my friends turned out to be insurance salesmen"[10]

Like the fish that jump out of puddles when the water level gets low, when I got out of the insurance business, I found so much freedom from the things I used to think I had to believe. I found out that the story was so vast and so much more complex than I'd ever imagined it to be. Rather than being used like currency with no will of my own, I got to be a part of what God was doing to make the world a place where righteousness is at home.[11]

It's always worth examining the story to see if it makes sense, to see where the trajectory is going, to see what the underlying plot is. Otherwise we can find ourselves telling a story to ourselves and others that exists simply to reinforce existing belief so that we never experience the discomfort of change or growth.

***

They say the last few miles of a marathon are more a mind game than anything else. I hadn't even gotten to the marathon hike I was

---

10 John Prine, "Illegal Smile." .
11 2 Peter 3:13 NRSV

training for, but the last few miles of an attempted sixteen-mile hike were definitely a mind game. My feet were hurting so bad, it was all I could do not to limp. My pacing was forgotten, and I just had to keep putting one foot in front of another. The beauty of the woods no longer existed for me. All I could see was the twelve-inch wide trail a few feet at a time in front of me. I was trudging. And I was miserable.

One piece of advice given to thru-hikers is "never quit on a bad day." I think the same could be said of all hiking. I got home seriously questioning my commitment to hike a full marathon. I couldn't imagine adding ten miles to what I had just done. And yet attempt it I must because I was raising money for Make-A-Wish, and I couldn't tell my donors who had been so generous and so supportive that I got to sixteen miles on a training hike and threw in the towel.

I sat on the couch with my feet up, scrolling Facebook and hating every hiking post I saw. Why did I think this was fun again? In that moment of pain, I couldn't remember. Beyond the pain from just being on my feet that long, I realized I had strained a tendon from repetitive use. So now in addition to trying to add miles, I needed to rehab this tendon so it didn't take me out of the game entirely.

Because I'd made a commitment, I kept up with my training and added the rehab on to my schedule. I went out and hiked a shorter, maintenance hike the next weekend to give my foot time to heal. And in a sunny moment beside one of my favorite streams, I heard the words, "always come back."

I chose to attempt the marathon because I thought it would be a good challenge for me while helping a bunch of kids get their wishes. I like having something to train for. Of course, having never attempted anything on that scale, I was unprepared for the fact that you can't train for a marathon without pain. Nor can you complete one without pain. Change and growth involve some degree of pain even if it's "good pain" like sore muscles and not the pain of an injury.

And again, I find life to be a lot like hiking. Ideally, we are always changing, always growing, and always seeking to push our former limits on how things can be. As we do this, more and more of what we thought was impossible becomes something we can grasp. Whether

Story

it's me attempting to hike 26.3 miles in one day, or making the world a more just and equitable place.

And a lot of whether we succeed or fail depends on the story we are telling ourselves about why we are doing what we are doing.

That place of awe, from which our contemplation of God begins, awaits us in the nooks and crannies of the natural world. Therefore, we must seek them out, soak them in, and care for them.
—Rabbi Jamie S. Korngold, *God in the Wilderness*, p. 60

15

Renewed

An unfamiliar dark blue car pulled slowly into the bottom of my driveway as I stood off to the side. There was an older man and woman inside, and I was pretty sure I'd never seen either of them before. The man rolled down the driver's side window and the woman leaned across him.

"Are you okay?" she asked.

I was startled out of my own thought space. "What? Yes, I'm okay."

And then I stopped to think about what I must have looked like, and started laughing. I was nine months pregnant with my second child and I had been having prodromal labor for weeks. Fairly intense contractions would hit sporadically throughout the day, and leave me exhausted. The contractions weren't moving to the active labor stage on their own, so I'd decided to do something about it. My mom had told a story about walking up a steep ramp when she was pregnant with my brother, and she was convinced that had started labor and led him to be born two weeks early. I figured it couldn't hurt, so I was walking up and down my insanely steep driveway, thirty-nine weeks pregnant and barefoot.

I was barefoot because I have more balance that way and I didn't want to fall. But seeing me down there, my hugely uncomfortable belly protruding over those bare feet, standing by the road with my phone in my hand, and I can see why they thought perhaps I was in distress of some kind. I mean, I was, but not the kind they could do anything about. Still, it's all too often that people see someone who might be in need and decide it's not any of their business, surely someone else will stop. But these folks took the time to make sure I was okay.

Both of my babies were stuck. I still don't know exactly why this was the case, but they both ended up requiring a surgical extraction. Probably it has something to do with my internal shape that can't really be seen or defined on ultrasounds or in exams, but the fact that both of them had similar difficulties coming out lends itself to that interpretation.

When I went into labor with my first, I was startled by the intensity of the contractions. I was sure it was going to go quickly, and I was more than a little nervous. I called my doula and begged her to come as soon as she could. She stayed with me all day and into the night as the contractions came and came and came and weren't building to the appropriate intensity.

By the second night, since my water had now been broken for twenty-four hours, I was in the hospital for observation and Pitocin. The contractions were so intense, and mostly in my back so my husband and my doula were taking turns providing much-needed counter-pressure on my back so I could get through them. I remember at one point in the darkest part of the night, feeling like I couldn't go on and that this would never end. I felt another contraction.

I murmured, "Here comes one," and neither of them moved. Both of them were asleep in their chairs. "Hey!" I got more insistent and they both started awake and jumped up. I felt bad for waking them, but I was the one in labor after all.

Even after almost forty hours of labor and four hours of pushing, he couldn't get out, so I ended up needing an emergency c-section. I'd worked diligently to avoid getting a c-section, feeling that surgical births are over performed, and there are some reasons at least to avoid it, not the least of which is recovering from a major surgery while caring for a newborn. But with the space and perspective that time brings as I look back on my birthing experiences, I realize that needing a community around me to birth these babies, then to help care for me and the new baby, as well as the difficulty and extreme amount of hard work involved in even bringing them into the world, is kind of the perfect metaphor for the shalom kingdom we are working to bring about.

Yes, birth as a metaphor is perhaps a little tired in some respects, and a literal, physical birth experience is one that not every member of our population can relate to. But the effort of bringing something new into the world—or working for renewal in our world—is something many of us participate in, and none of us can do alone.

I have a friend who lives in a historic neighborhood in Nashville. She organized her neighbors to beautify their street. And then the next street over. Imagine if more of us did that. Just one person, bringing together a few more people, focused on whatever little spot of this world we have influence over. But what does that look like on a day to day basis?

***

The little bush that volunteered next to my shed had pretty dark green leaves on it. It snuggled up next to the shed, wrapping itself around the corner. I liked the effect, and so I left it to grow. In my mind, that was letting the forest "come back" to an area that had previously been cleared. I'd noticed another little bush like it at the bottom of the driveway. Then after we cut down a damaged white pine a few years ago, several more of the same kind of bush sprang up. I still wasn't suspicious, until I went on a plant identification spree and learned that this pretty little bush with the dark green leaves was an invasive species called privet. It reproduces faster than the trees and shrubs that are native to this area and will outcompete them for nutrients. We cut the pretty bush by the shed down, and are methodically removing the other ones springing up as well. If we take out ours, in addition to preserving the forest on our own land, we help prevent the spread of these plants to the land around ours too.

The park I hike at regularly and many other state parks in the area host "clean up days" not to pick up trash as much as to remove invasive species to reclaim our forests from things that would otherwise choke them out. Privet, one form of the popular landscaping plant known as "burning bush," as well as a vining species that produces pretty white flowers can together decimate a native forest.

It seems like invasive species should be ugly, should be recognizable, should scream "I don't belong here," but all of the common invasive species around me are outwardly beautiful. You have to learn about them, and learn to recognize them to see the harm hidden beneath the flowers and attractive foliage.

***

As I write this, spring has sprung. In many past years, this would mean appreciating the forsythia I planted when my oldest was a baby, and waiting for the daffodils that I put in the garden to emerge. The daffodils were a house warming present thirteen years ago, and when they stopped blooming in their pot, I transferred them to a few places in the garden where they have faithfully emerged each spring in larger numbers. The forsythia I found on a discount table at a garden shop. It had stopped blooming and was just a few shoots of green leaves on gangly twigs no more than a foot tall and maybe eight inches wide. It's now taller than I am and covers the entire five foot width on the side of my back porch and then some.

I've always thought that planting things for spring requires a lot of faith and patience. Spring bulbs must be planted in the fall. It takes planning and foresight and yes, faith, to believe that these dried lumpy bits buried in the earth are going to do anything other than decompose. It takes faith to believe the earth is a womb and not a tomb.

A few weeks ago as I hiked through my favorite park on a day when the sky was a leaden shade of gray and felt just as heavy, it would have been easy to believe that this was all there was. That the sound of my footfalls on the rocks and earth meant there was nothing else living in this forest. The only other sounds were the occasional rustling of the leaves as the wind stirred them, and here and there a ghostly moan as tree branches rubbed together. These shades of brown and gray, the dead leaves that crunched under foot, the skeletal sentinels of the sleeping trees combined to create the impression that I was the only living thing in those woods. And indeed, starting as early as I had that morning, I went at least six miles or so without seeing anyone else, making me realize that as much as I like hiking alone, the occasional "good morning" from other hikers is an important lift to my spirits.

On the trail the leaves get crushed by foot traffic, and at some point the bare earth and rock re-emerges. But on either side, the leaves sit several inches deep, quietly decomposing until the line between what is leaf and what is soil is non-existent. The leaves are the original mulch, protecting the ground. Of course, if you brush them aside in the midst of winter, all you'll find is bare earth. It's not obvious in the winter what the leaves are protecting.

Yesterday, I hiked my favorite route through the park and as I got a few miles in, starting my descent to the first creek crossing, I stopped in wonder. The entire hillside was covered in blue and yellow flowers: ragwort and phlox. As I descended to the valley the creek runs through, they were joined by Valerian and dwarf larkspur with trilliums sprouting around the edges. The entire understory was awash in color. Birdsong trickled down from the treetops above. Delirious bees bounced from flower to flower buzzing drunkenly, harvesting the abundance around them, and spreading life with their feet.

The air was lightly perfumed. Not heavy-handed like the overwhelming artificial fragrances that leave chemtrails in their wake as you pass by people wearing them, but just enough to tint the breeze as it brushed by me on its way down the valley. The dead leaves had yielded to a plethora of green and yellow and blue and purple interspersed with splashes of red and deep burgundy. There is no way to fully capture it: not here in these words, nor in the many pictures I snapped as I moved slowly, filled with wonder.

It's Saturday of Holy Week, and I'm treading slowly through these words, looking around to see if I've wrapped everything up the way one expects to at the end of a book. But then I wonder if that's even the right way to think about it. This book is a snapshot of my thoughts at this time. There's bound to be things that change even as soon as I send it to the publisher. And this book is right now mostly a monologue in that until you picked it up, it was a one-sided conversation. But you did pick it up, and now you get to fill in your part.

Undergoing a crisis of faith, wrapping myself in that chrysalis of transformation, emerging to find there's more to unpack and more to unlearn, but also so much more to discover and more to embrace, has shown me that this work is ongoing and sometimes cyclical. As much as we want it to be linear, to be logical, the reality is messy and mystifying, and often far more than we can explain.

Saturday of Holy Week is the Easter Vigil, where we have a late service, and a bonfire where we burn the palms from Palm Sunday.

The ashes will be mixed with oil for next Ash Wednesday to make smudged crosses on the foreheads of the faithful. Ash Wednesday and the tomb bridge the flowers and the celebration of Easter morning.

The palms we wave become the ashes to start the next lent. The leaves fall from the trees and protect the soil that will feed the next wave of spring flowers. The soil rests through the dark, long nights of winter, preparing for new life, just as my children grew in the dark secret space of my womb.

The ashes and the decaying leaves and the cells knitting together at the microscopic level are just the start. The waiting in the dark, the pain and the labor: it's all part of the resurrection. We don't get the resurrection without the cross. We don't get spring without winter. We don't get life without death. Each cycle builds on the one before it, reminding us that we are working for new life, but at the same time, awaiting our own ultimate resurrection.

Protecting the forest in the park from invasive plants has preserved an understory that is both beautiful and nourishing. It's an ongoing labor, but with each year that passes, the forest returns stronger than ever. But like the mess that creeps back in my house every time I've put my head into my writing, guarding against invasive plants in the forest is an ongoing job. There are properties where the invasive plants are being planted as landscaping, where they are being welcomed as a good thing, where people ignore the warnings.

The Bradford pear is a particularly good example of this. It's available at many of the big box store gardening centers and people plant them in multiples around their houses. These trees seed themselves into sections that have been cleared and are taking over from the native pear tree. They grow fast, which is one of the reasons people like them. But these fast growing interlopers are also very weak. After any decently strong storm, you can find some of them broken on the ground somewhere. It would be far better to be patient with our landscaping choice, and to cultivate plants that are slower and more complex than to opt for the fast and easy and brittle.

***

I once believed the forest of my faith wasn't worth saving. But as I began to pull the invasive species of doctrine and wade deeper into the old growth, I discovered a rich ecosystem that is life-giving, diverse, and worth exploring. It took me a while to see the invasive species weren't the forest, that they could be discarded without clear-cutting anything. And once those invasive species were gone, I could see things more like how they ought to be: complex and diverse and freeing.

Last fall to my delight, I found asters that had sowed themselves on the border of the cut edge of my yard. Each spring, clover that we've sown crops up interspersed with buttercups, chickweed, and dandelions that have sown themselves. While we do mow a portion of it, we haven't made our yard into a lawn.

When we first built our house here, most of the road was still farmland. Slowly over the past thirteen years, especially in the last five, the pastures full of flowers and cows have been replaced by McMansion-style dwellings fronted by large swaths of nothing but grass. I can only imagine these uniform acres of green cost a lot of money to achieve. And then there's the cost that is initially hidden: the cost to the bees and the ecosystem. The bees need those first flowers of spring, and the ecosystem doesn't need the chemicals used to keep up those uniform expanses.

Uniform is simpler though. You only have to learn about one kind of plant. If you declare that this is the only kind of plant that gets to grow here, then you don't have to examine or learn about the other plants, you just have to exterminate them. All difference is a threat to the desired uniformity.

It takes time and effort to learn about all the different plants in an ecosystem and learn to care for each of them in the unique way they need. Even forests need care, especially in the removal of invasive species. Yes, they have their own ways and means but to truly thrive they must be protected from destructive pests both plant and insect.

So too with my faith, it's been fascinating to see what grew when I plucked the invasive and destructive beliefs out of the forest. What I discovered was much more vast and complex and wild than I could ever have imagined.

Empire seeks to make everything uniform and subdued to best serve the interests of the few in power. American mythology rides on taming as a positive influence. The idea that the European settlers needed to tame the wild land and civilize the wild people for their own good allowed the justification at the heart of the genocide and land grab that made space for the beginnings of this country.

Then we had cowboy mythology and the taming of the "wild" west. Wherever you turn, taming is part of creating the American myth. Taming is presented as the work of civilization. So we tame people into widgets and forests into lawns and ourselves into pale imitations of our potential because we believe that's what the American empire-god wants.

In reality, it's the wild that needs to be protected both in ourselves and in our world. It's the wild that's under attack because the wild won't conform. The wild whose complexity and diversity has been misunderstood, exploited, and all too often, eradicated has much to offer us. The wild in ourselves and in our world must be tended: a lesson we can once again learn from the first peoples to inhabit these lands.

It's not too late. We can undertake a life of pilgrimage, become thru-hikers through our world and our stories, and rediscover the wild spirit we all came into this world with. We can clear the invasive species and doctrines and reclaim our forests and our souls.

Miles are made up of steps; personal change begins with small commitments; and social change begins with individuals. At the beginning of a long hike, the miles stretching out in front of me can feel overwhelming, but I've discovered that if I just start—if I just get moving—then once I've got a few miles in, the distance becomes more manageable. And while the first four or five miles might feel like a big undertaking, when I have ten or so miles under my belt, the last few miles don't seem nearly as long. Each tiny step adds up, and the force of the miles I've already hiked pushes me forward. It helps me to remember this each time I am overwhelmed by the brokenness of the world: all I have to do is begin. There's no such thing as too small an action to make a difference as long as we commit to consistency. All we have to do is begin.

Renewed

Acknowledgments

We think of writing as a solitary affair, but in my experience, it's not. So to everyone who helped bring this book into the world, thank you! I've learned like so many other things, I can't write a book by myself. This book is dedicated to and exists because of these people.

My husband, Jody, who listened to so many sections and rants and ideas and who also fed me while I was finishing the manuscript: I might not still be here without you, and I love this adventure we're on.

My kids, Eli and August, who were very understanding of sharing their mom with her book-baby: I hope you read this one day and decide it was worth it. I'm trying to do my part to make the world you inherit a better place.

Shari, who spent the better part of two years hearing about this in conversation and helped me tweak the end to be that much better: both the book and I owe you a lot.

Amy, who read the entire first draft and offered much insight: the final version owes much to you, my friend.

Yejide, who kept cheering for this to exist when I had my doubts: thank you for believing in me when I didn't.

The entire Global Writer's Group sponsored by Freedom Road and dreamed up by Lisa Sharon Harper. The members of this group help each other find our unique voices and I'm so grateful to be a part of that.

And thank you to Matthew Wimer and the team at Wipf and Stock for taking a chance on this book and bringing it to the world.

Bibliography

Bolz Weber, Nadia. *Accidental Saints*. New York: Convergent Books, 2015.

———. "While it was still dark" https://www.redletterchristians.org/while-it-was-still-dark-a-requiem-for-rachel-held-evans/. Accessed April 6, 2022.

Brown, Austin Channing. *I'm Still Here: Black Dignity in a World Made for Whiteness*. New York: Convergent, 2018.

Brown, Brené. *I Thought It Was Just Me (but it isn't)*. New York: Gotham Books, 2007.

Bruggemann, Walter. *An Introduction to the Old Testament*. Louisville: Westminster John Knox, 2003.

———., Walter C. Kaiser, Leander E. Keck, Terence E. Fretheim. *The New Interpreter's Bible: A Commentary in Twelve Volumes. Volume I: General and Old Testament Articles, Genesis, Exodus, Leviticus*. Nashville: Abingdon Press, 1994.

———. *Prophetic Imagination*. Minneapolis: Fortress, 2001.

CDC. "Sexual Violence is Preventable." Accessed April 4, 2022. https://www.cdc.gov/injury/features/sexual-violence/index.html

Chu, Jeff. *Does Jesus Really Love Me?* New York: Harper Perennial, 2013.

Curtice, Kaitlin B. *Native: Identity, Belonging, and Rediscovering God*. Grand Rapids: Brazos, 2020.

———. Facebook post March 21, 2022, accessed April 4, 2022 https://www.Facebook.com/1674085646191456/posts/3171969159736423/?d=n

Doyle, Glennon. *Untamed*. New York: The Dial Press, 2020.

Elliot, Elisabeth. *A Time to Die*. Grand Rapids: Revell, 1987.

Finer, Lawrence B., Lori F. Frohwirth, Lindsay A. Dauphinee, Susheela Singh, Ann M. Moore. "Reasons U.S. Women Have Abortions: Quantitative and Qualitative Perspectives." *Guttmacher Institute* 37, Issue 3 (September 2005): 110-118. https://www.guttmacher.org/journals/psrh/2005/reasons-us-women-have-abortions-quantitative-and-qualitative-perspectives

Green, Joel B. *The Gospel of Luke*. Grand Rapids: Eerdmans, 1997.

Gilbert, Jack. *Collected Poems*. New York: Alfred A. Knopf, 2021.

Gilliard, Dominique. *Subversive Witness: Scripture's Call to Leverage Privilege*. Grand Rapids: Zondervan, 2021.

Harper, Lisa Sharon. *Fortune: How Race Broke My Family and the World and How to Repair it All*. Grand Rapids: Brazos, 2022.

____. *The Very Good Gospel*. New York: Waterbrook, 2016.

Harper, Lisa Sharon and René August. "How to Decolonize the Bible." Freedom Road Institute, April 2020. https://freedomroad.us/downloads/how-to-decolonize-the-bible-webinar/.

Henry, Andre. *All the White Friends I Couldn't Keep*. New York: Convergent, 2022.

Heschel, Abraham Joshua. *The Sabbath*. New York: Farrar, Straus, and Giroux, 1951.

hooks, bell. *All About Love*. New York: William Morrow, 2001.

Howard, Anna Elisabeth. "The God Who Sees Me." February 21, 2021. https://aehowardwrites.substack.com/p/the-god-who-sees-me.

____. "Things Done and Left Undone: the Confession as a Call to Right Relationship." *Earth & Altar*. September 28, 2021. https://earthandaltarmag.com/posts/eygvsgi1i2czkbxsss9xgyvd6lfby. Accessed May 5, 2022.

____. "Poisoned Bible Project 1: Does God Hate Women?" May 1, 2021. https://aehowardwrites.substack.com/p/does-god-hate-women-poisoned-bible.

____. "Seeking Shalom: Moving from Entropy to Equity." *Earth and Altar*. April 18, 2022. https://earthandaltarmag.com/posts/ujah647erwirmcyoqkfenhlmzxqg4s

Jackson, Peter, director, 2002. *The Two Towers*. New Line Cinema.

Johnson, Elizabeth A. *She Who Is*. New York: Herder and Herder, 2002.

Kenny, Amy. *My Body is Not a Prayer Request*. Grand Rapids: Brazos, 2022.

Kidd, Sue Monk. *The Dance of the Dissident Daughter*. New York: Harper Collins, 1996.

Kimmerer, Robin Wall. *Braiding Sweetgrass*. Minneapolis: Milkweed Editions, 2013.

Korngold, Jamie S. *God in the Wilderness*. New York: Doubleday, 2008.

Lewis, C.S. *The Last Battle*. New York: Harper Collins, 2004.

Menakem, Resmaa. *My Grandmothers Hands*. Las Vegas: Central Recovery Press, 2017.

Oliver, Mary. *Devotions: The Selected Poems*. New York: Penguin, 2017.

Oswalt, John N. *The Book of Isaiah: Chapters 40-66*. Grand Rapids: Eerdmans, 1998.

Parts Unknown. Season 11, Episode 1 "West Virginia." Directed by Morgan Fallon. Aired April 29, 2018 on CNN.

Pasquale, Teresa B. *Healing Spiritual Wounds*. St. Louis: Chalice Press, 2015.

Prine, John. "Illegal Smile." Track 1. *John Prine*. Atlantic Records, 1971.

Renkl, Margaret. *Late Migrations: A Natural History of Love and Loss*. Minneapolis: Milkweed Editions, 2019.

Rowling, J.K. *Harry Potter and the Deathly Hallows*. New York: Arthur A. Levine, 2007.

Shetler, Kaitlin. "Burning Bush." "Emmaus." "Judas." Published on Facebook. https://www.Facebook.com/kaitlinhardyshetler/. Used by permission.

Shire, Warsan. "Home." *Bless the Daughter Raised by a Voice in her Head*. New York: Random House, 2022.

Steenland, Sally. "The Religious Right Wasn't Created to Battle Abortion." *Center for American Progress*. March 27, 2013. https://www.americanprogress.org/article/the-religious-right-wasnt-created-to-battle-abortion/. Accessed May 9, 2022.

Solzhenitsyn, Alexander. *The Gulag Archipelago*. New York: Collins, 1974.

Sonderegger, Katherine. *Systematic Theology, Volume 1, The Doctrine of God*. Minneapolis: Fortress Press, 2015.

Taylor, Helen. *Little Pilgrim's Progress*. Chicago: Moody Bible Institute, 2006.

Thornton, Russell. "Cherokee Population Losses during the Trail of Tears: A New Perspective and a New Estimate." *Ethnohistory 31*, no. 4 (1984): 289–300. https://doi.org/10.2307/482714.

Tippet, Krista. Interview with Ruby Sales. *On Being*. Podcast audio. September 15, 2016. https://onbeing.org/programs/ruby-sales-where-does-it-hurt/.

Tolkein, J.R.R. *The Silmarillion*. New York: Haughton Mifflin, 2004.

Treisman, Rachel. "California Program Giving $500 No-Strings-Attached Stipends Pays Off, Study Finds." NPR. March 4, 2021, https://www.npr.org/2021/03/04/973653719/california-program-giving-500-no-strings-attached-stipends-pays-off-study-finds, accessed May 14, 2022.

U2. "Walk On." Track 4. *All that You Can't Leave Behind*. Interscope Records, 2000.

Volf, Miroslav. *Free of Charge: Giving and Forgiving in a Culture Stripped of Grace*. Grand Rapids: Zondervan, 2005.

Woodley, Randy. *Becoming Rooted*. Minneapolis: Broadleaf, 2022.

Younge, Gary. "Working Class Voters: Why America's Poor are Willing to Vote Republican." *The Guardian*. Oct 29, 2012. https://www.theguardian.com/world/2012/oct/29/working-class-voters-america-republican. Accessed 6/26/2021.

About the Author

Anna Elisabeth Howard writes highly caffeinated takes on shalom as a lens for everything from her front porch in Hendersonville, TN where she lives with her husband and two sons and a small menagerie of critters. She is a community organizer and movement chaplain with a background in youth and family ministry and is a graduate of Fuller Theological Seminary. An avid hiker and backpacker, many thoughts start somewhere in the middle of the woods or under a waterfall.

www.ingramcontent.com/pod-product-compliance
Lightning Source LLC
Chambersburg PA
CBHW070742160426
43192CB00009B/1546